The Frazier Chronicles

Stories Untold: Finding Peace After Pain

Compiled by Jai the Author Publishing

Copyright © 2016 Jai the Author Publishing. All Rights Reserved. Each story found within is property of the individual writers. The dedication, final note and afterword were written by Jamie "Jai" Hopkins. Jai the Author Publishing is the Publisher on Record and holds the copyright to the book in its entirety.

ISBN: 0692810145
ISBN-13: 978-0692810149

Contents

Foreword 3

Dedication 4

The Frazier Family History 9

Section 1: Behind Closed Doors 15
Martha A. Harris (Frazier) 16
TeResa L. Frazier-Johnson 20
Jamie Y. Hopkins 26
Katrina M. Brown 39
Josie L. Hopkins 50
Sherika J. Shedwick 58
Vanessa D. Fryer 66

Section 2: Finding True Love 75
Angela R. Frazier 76

Section 3: When Life Unexpectedly Throws You a Curve Ball 91
Sharalene D. Frazier 92
Shanelle D. Frazier 97

Final Note from the Authors 109

Afterword 110

About the Publisher 111

The *Frazier* Chronicles

Foreword

Written by Commander Gervaise A. Williams, United States Navy [Retired]

The Frazier Chronicles is a telling anthology revealing the most intimate secrets of ten women in their attempt to escape the chains of bondage that have held them captive for years. The resilience displayed by these ladies is a true testament to their character and faith in God, as well as themselves. Mind you, they are not alone in their experiences as there are countless instances of emotional, sexual, and physical abuse experienced by our women of color. However, they have displayed a level of intestinal fortitude and strength that is indicative of the BLACK WOMAN.

As you read this anthology, you, no matter your gender, station in life, or current situation, will be moved and encouraged to let YOUR SECRETS be revealed so that you, too, can effectively embark upon your own journey of emotional healing. The journey will not be easy as you will have to deal with a myriad of insecurities, fears, and possibly even self-doubt. However, I assure you, it will be worth it in the end.

To the ladies of *The Frazier Chronicles*, my hat goes off to you. I know, as I have conversed with most of you, the degree of difficulty you endured in coming to grips with your pain as a result of the events shared in this anthology. Nonetheless, you persevered and found the strength to convey your individual messages. I assure you, it will not be for naught. Not only will you touch others through your selfless display of courage, but more importantly, YOU HAVE TOUCHED EACH OTHER! Keep in mind the journey has just begun, but TOGETHER you are healing. A true testament to FAMILY. You GO, ladies!

Dedication

Minnie Lee O'Neal (Frazier)
1939 - 2014

I could never tell my grandmother's story. Most of it, she never told herself. And most of the players in her story have long passed away. So all I have are memories, and we all know how reliable and unreliable they can be.

Mrs. Minnie Lee O'Neal (Frazier) was one of the sweetest, no-nonsense women I knew! She was soft-spoken, loving, always smiling, and always thought the best of people. Though she was soft-spoken in spirit she had the loudest outside voice ever! You could clearly hear her distinct voice all the way down the street, and she was just telling you blow by blow of what happened on her favorite soap opera.

Everyone called her "Miss Minnie". Oh, and when I tell you she could throw down in the kitchen… she was the best cook ever! Of course, I'm a little bias because she's my grandmother.

One thing I remember the most about my grandmother was that she was the most forgiving. She pardoned a lot of wrongs done to her and to her loved ones; and she was quick to tell you that you deserved to be treated with decency and respect. She always wanted the best for her children and her grandchildren.

Family <u>always</u> came first. She preached that every chance she got. She was serious and didn't care if we liked it or not. She stood her ground. And when she gave us "that look", or she sighed really hard, we knew not to push the envelope.

In one of my writings, I tell the story of the time my grandmother received those small cut marks on her arms by the man she was cohabiting with at the time. He was a diabetic drunk with one leg, and he was abusive to my grandmother and her small grandchildren. He would only terrorize the grandkids when our parents were not home by chasing us around the house with his wooden leg. When we told our parents, they would take that wooden leg and beat the sh*t out of him with it.

Though I have many, many memories with my grandmother, the ones I choose to cherish are the good ones that did not involve her being physically abused by her intimate partners. The physical violence on my grandmother ceased and desisted when she met and married the only man I will ever call my grandfather: Mr. Virgil "VO" O'Neal.

(NOTE: I never met Jerry Frazier since he passed away when I was young and they had long divorced by then. Sad to say that I've never met—or remember meeting—his other children, whom are my aunts and uncles, their children, or children's children.)

When my grandmother met and married V.O., her life took on a whole new meaning. Her home became the family gathering place for all holidays, cookouts, hangouts, fish fry's, etc. Family was everything to her, and there was a lot of us! Anyone who came through her door was fed. She believed in feeding people. Everything would be okay with a southern home cooked meal. She was the best cook anyway, and everyone knew it.

We weren't the perfect family though. We weren't the perfect kids or grandkids. Our choices caused a great deal of disappointment to my grandmother, because she always wanted the best for us. We just didn't want that for ourselves. But no matter how disappointed she was with some of our decisions, she never turned us away. She never treated us differently. She remained the sweetest, kindest, most loving mother and grandmother ever.

Teenage pregnancy, marrying one abusive drunk after the other, high school dropouts, teen running away from home to live with a man old enough to be grandfather, stealing items out of her house to sell to buy liquor or drugs, bickering and fighting with one another, moving out of State and not checking in with family, depending on welfare and food stamps with no ambition for a better life, succumbing to alcohol and drug addiction, running behind these knuckle-head-good-for-nothing boys or hot-in-the-pants girls… oh, the list goes on. Not to mention her own daughters walking around with blackened eyes, busted lips, broken limbs, hospitalized from the abuse… yeah, my grandmother had a lot of heartache caused by her kids, grandkids, and great-grandkids. We put her through! But she never shut us out. She stepped in and would talk to us, give us words of encouragement, tell us that God wanted much more for us. She was the matriarch of the family. She was our savior in so many ways. And we all took her for granted while she was alive.

Again, the thing I remember the most about my grandmother, other than her beautiful salt-and-pepper colored hair, was her ability to forgive. She was the most forgiving woman, no matter how horrible of a human being you displayed in front of her. She always looked past our faults and saw our need to be forgiven and loved. Now, don't get it wrong, she was a no-nonsense type of chick! She had an opinion about everything and wasn't afraid to call you out on your bullsh*t; but it always came from a place of good intentions.

My grandmother taught us that forgiveness was not about forgetting the wrong or the one who wronged us, it was about being free and setting boundaries and limitations so the wrong didn't <u>continue</u>. We could forgive someone without having them in our lives; but we had a responsibility to be a good-hearted person. A God-fearing person. That was our responsibility and obligation after all God had done for our family.

My grandmother never kicked anyone out of her life completely though. Even the man who left those scars on her body for life eternity, when she finally left him, she still looked after him. When he was found dead butt naked in his boarding room, my grandmother was the one who made funeral arrangements for him, against her children's wishes. She kept saying that she felt sorry for him and no one should have to die alone. That's my grandmother… always caring for every and anybody, no matter how badly they behaved.

So there you have it, the lesson that rings throughout this entire book and in all of our stories: learning to forgive yourself and others. The key to a pain free, emotionally healed life: FORGIVE.

Bone cancer took my grandmother away from us. Heaven gained an angel on August 28, 2014! Gone, but never ever forgotten. We love you! We pray that you are smiling in Heaven as you look down upon us.

Jai at her grandmother's grave in 2015

The Frazier Family History

Many years ago, our ancestors were brought here to the United States from Nigeria, West Africa. They were sold as slaves to the Frazier's Plantation. We don't know what their names were at that time, however, all slaves were given the last name of their slave holders. From this lot, Sylvester Frazier was born to the parents of Tom and Carrie Frazier.

Sylvester later met and married Martha Price. Sylvester and Martha were God-fearing people who believed the words "be fruitful and multiply", and multiply they did! In the year of 1956, and in the month of October, God saw fit that Sylvester should depart his earthly life.

The practice of multiplication was passed on and on. Sylvester and Martha had nine Frazier children, which make up the first generation: Jerry, Charles, Stella, Clara, Lennel, Mary, Carrie, James and Curtis.

Jerry Frazier, the oldest of the first generation, married three times and had eleven children! One of his wives was Minnie Lee, who became the matriarch of this very compilation you are reading now. The next to the oldest, Charles Frazier, fondly known as "Uncle Pete", had nine children, of whom the youngest is included in this compilation.

So, in essence, this anthology consists of second and third generations of the Frazier clan.

The *Frazier* Chronicles

The Frazier Family Tree (abbreviated)

pink boxes indicate the lineages included in this compilation

First Generation of Fraziers

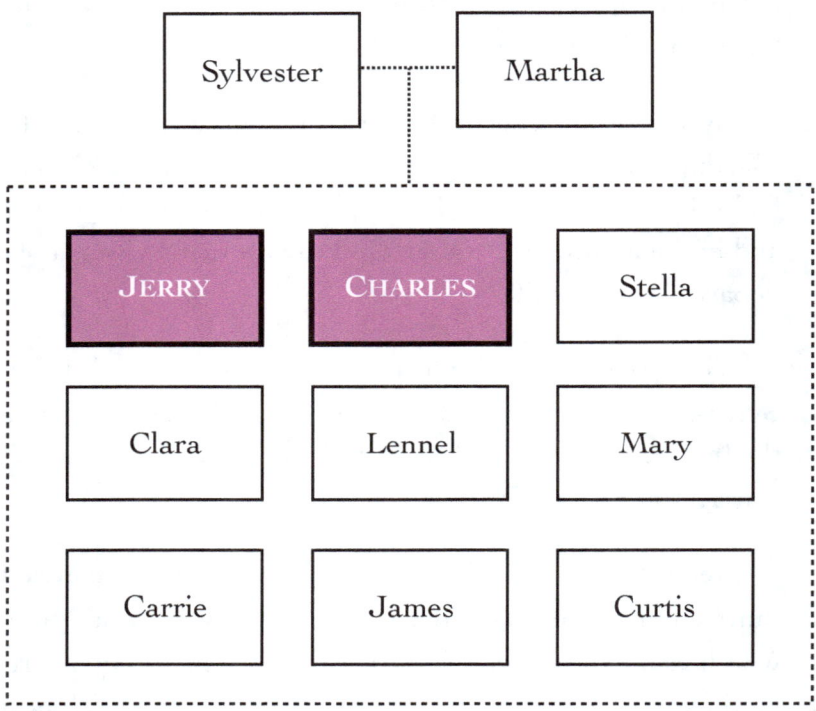

Second Generation of Fraziers

Jerry Frazier's first wife was our grandmother, Mrs. Minnie Lee, and they had four children.

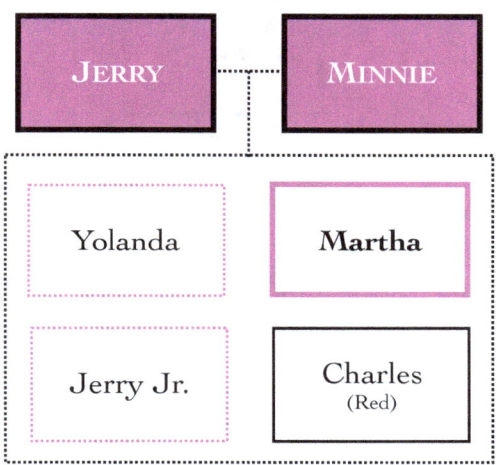

Jerry was married two other times and fathered seven more children.

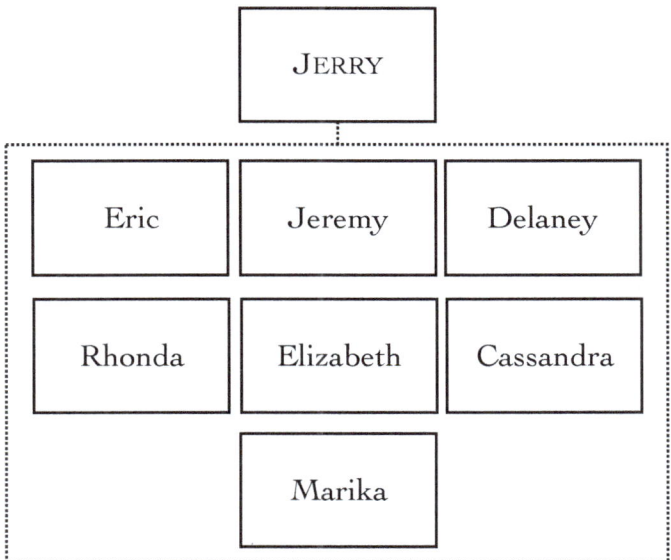

THE *Frazier* CHRONICLES

Second Generation of Fraziers (cont'd)

Minnie Lee and her brother-in-law's children shown below

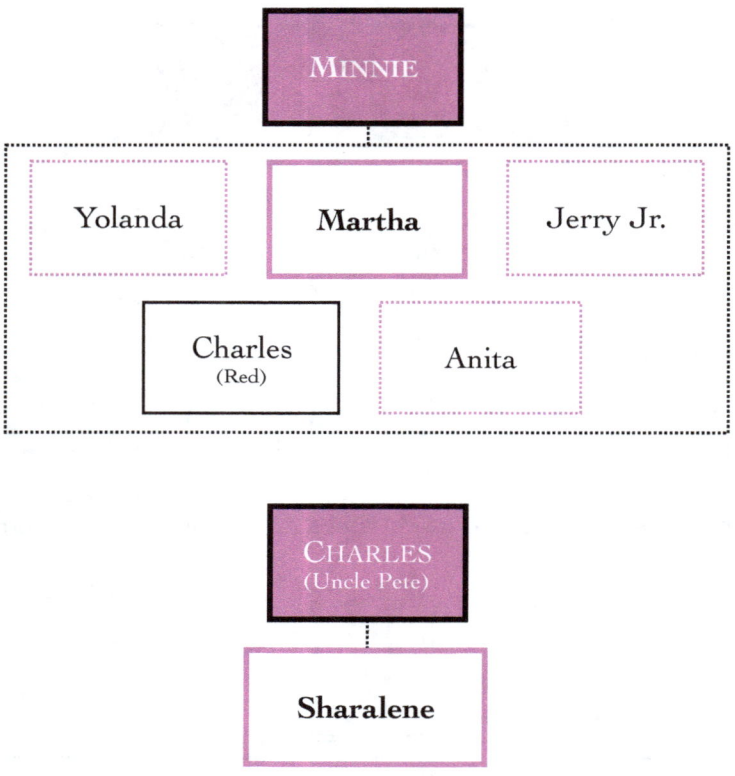

**spouses & other siblings not included, only the contributors in this anthology

Third Generation of Fraziers

Minnie Lee's grandchildren shown below

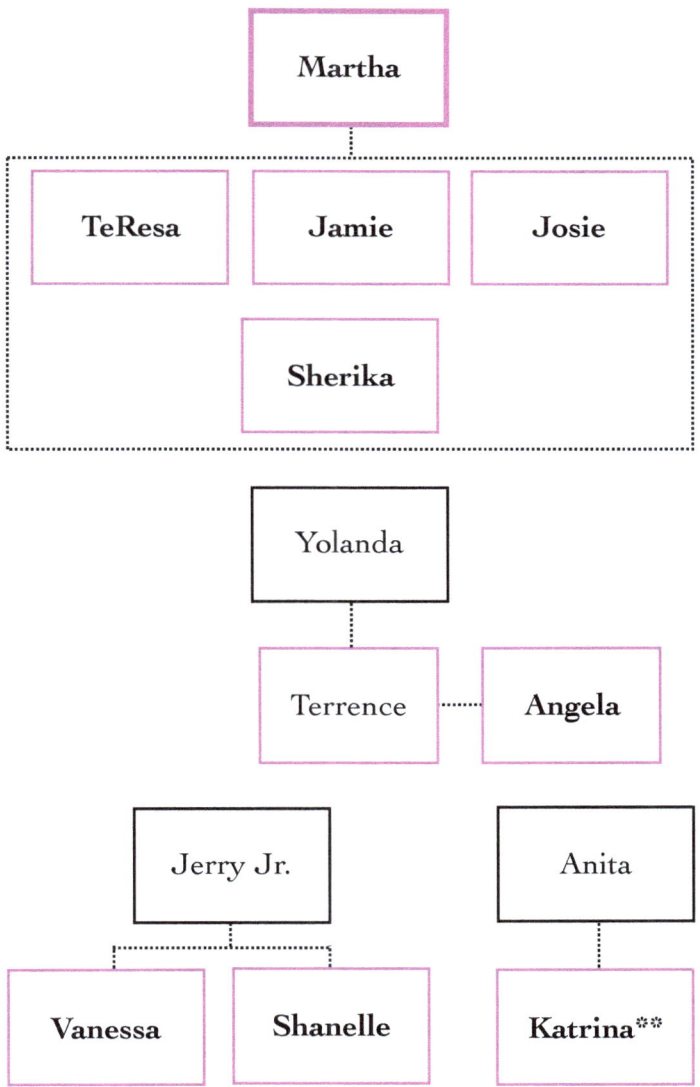

*spouses & other siblings not included, only contributors in this anthology
**Katrina was adopted & raised by her aunt, Martha

THE *Frazier* CHRONICLES

THE Frazier CHRONICLES

Section 1: Behind Closed Doors

NOTE: The names of our abusers have been changed for the sake of confidentiality as well as our own journey of forgiveness and emotional healing.

"Someone was hurt before you, wronged before you, hungry before you, frightened before you, beaten before you, humiliated before you, raped before you... yet, someone survived... You can do anything you choose to do." Maya Angelou

Chapter One

Martha is on the right.

Martha A. Harris (Frazier)

#MommaBear
My Life, My Story

My life has not always been peaches and cream. I got pregnant at a very early age. Dropped out of high school. I got married and moved out of my mother's house because I didn't want to obey her rules. I had a very abusive step father. He would fight my mom every weekend when he drank.

I was only 16 years old but I knew that's not the kind of relationship I wanted for myself. After maybe two years, my husband became verbally abusive. Nothing I did satisfied him. He was the only provider for our family, and I was a stay-at-home mom. But then I decided to go back to school and get a job.

Things were fine for a while. I started making more money than him and the marriage started going downhill. He became a monster. The abuse turned physical—black eye, busted lips, hair pulled out. I was a prisoner in my own home. I had to ask for permission to go anywhere. Then I had to give definite times when I would be back home. If I was five minutes late, it was a fight.

After one Saturday night of fighting and crying, I went to church the next Sunday morning. As the preacher was giving his sermon, he was looking straight at me. Every bone in my body hurt. All I could do was cry. I knew God was speaking to me through him. I had enough. I went home, packed me and my children's clothes and left. Not knowing where we were going, I just knew I couldn't stay there any longer.

I continued to work and provide for my children. They did not have what they wanted, but they always had what they needed. Sometime later, I met another man that showed me love and affection. I just knew he was the one the Lord had sent me to help care for my family. Lord, I could not have been more wrong!

When we were dating, he was wonderful. After we got married, all hell broke loose. He was abusive to me and my children. He would hit me in front of them so that he would have a reason to hit them. I know in my heart that was the reason why my children left home. At the time, I felt like I needed a man in my life. I didn't want to be alone.

As the sixteen years went by, I prayed and prayed and asked the Lord to remove me from this life. I would rather be dead than to live like this. I was supposed to live the life I wanted my girls to have someday. This was not it.

In 1998, I suffered a heart attack. I thought this was God saying, "Ok, it's time." I thought He was finally answering my prayer to take me out of this world. But God spared me because He had something better for me to do. When I came home from the hospital, I had to live with my parents because my husband would not care for me. When I got well enough to return home, I said to myself, "That's it. I don't need a man like this."

The abuse stopped. The communication stopped. The wifey duties stopped. We were like two strangers in the same house. I did not talk, cook or wash for him since that day. One day he tried to pick a fight, and I called the police to have him removed from my home! Yes, MY home. When I bought it, I made sure only my name was on the deed because I knew this day was coming.

After my second divorce, I stayed single for three years. Happy and content with my new life. The Lord had blessed me with a good paying job. I had worked for a very wonderful boss for ten years, and when he retired, he sold me the business. I am now a business owner!!! I am still in awe at all God had done after all the abuse I went through. Many nights of not knowing what would happen to me or my children, and now I own a thriving accounting firm. I continue to give God all of the praise and glory!

On August 23, 2007, the Lord called my daddy, V.O., home. That was the saddest day in my life. He was the kindest, most generous man I had ever known. He would give you the shirt off of his back. I mourn him today. He will always be in my heart. Yes, Jerry Frazier is my biological father; but V.O. was the one that picked up the mantle of being the best daddy a girl could ask for! When he died, a part of me died too.

Then on March 6, 2009, God sent me a very Godly man. He has so many traits of my daddy. He's caring, funny, loving, and a good provider too. He's a family man. The Lord took one good man out of my life and replaced him with another. Lord, I thank You!

I have never been happier. He adores my children. He will give them the shirt off of his back. As you can see, although my life is perfect now, I have had some trials and tribulations that the Lord brought me through. If He did it for me, He will do the same for you. Trust and believe. That's all He asks.

Abuse (verbal or physical) is not to be taken lightly. It is an epidemic that's plaguing our society. It destroys families. It affects our mental stability. If you are a victim, please tell someone. It can be a family member or a total stranger. You are NOT ALONE.

Martha Ann

(also known as "Momma" or "Madear")

"Nothing is impossible, the word itself says I'm Possible!" Audrey Hepburn

Chapter Two

TeResa L. Frazier – Johnson

#daOldest
Speak Up and Speak Out

Before I begin, I would like to give reverence to God, who is the Creator and Vision of this family project. He has been the Source and Provider Who has permitted us to share our stories with the world.

When asked to participate in this family project, I immediately became excited and I thought of everything that I could include in my "conversation piece." Then it settled in on me. I thought, "Can I really say that?" or "I don't think it's time to tell this yet!" Then I realized the purpose of this project: to break our silence of abuse that has been in our family for almost one hundred years. So, now it's my turn to break free from the things that have held me hostage for years.

Since forever, I have put blame to the past as to why and how I do things in life. During my childhood, I could remember so plainly when my parents would physically fight over something that seems so unimportant now. For years, my sisters and I had to listen to them argue and fight all night long. I cried many nights and wished I could click my heels together (like Dorothy from the Wizard of Oz) and go to another place far, far away. I felt tired and worried at an early age. I was tired of the fights, tired of getting up in the middle of the night to go to Grandma's house, just tired. I knew even back then, this was no way to live.

I saw my Momma hold jobs that were not of her character. She went to college and landed a somewhat of a good job with a management company. Momma kept us fed, even if she didn't eat. We didn't understand until years later why she would do and say the things that she did. SHE LOVED US!! SHE PROTECTED US!! SHE GAVE US LIFE!! I thank God that us girls had sense enough to know that we did not want to endure the things that Momma did, so we all, by God's grace, went off and finished school (high school was good enough for Momma), some of us got really good jobs, nice homes, and so forth. But the trail of abuse came back into our lives…one by one.

I'm not quite sure of the years or how old I was, but it began when I was a young child. There were times when my mom had to go out of town, either for work or school, and we were left home with my dad. There were a few times when I was awakened late at night and led into the room where my parents slept. I didn't understand what was happening at the time, but I knew it was not supposed to happen between me and him. As I began to cry, he slapped me. I screamed and he put his hand over my mouth. I told him that I was going to tell Momma and he said that he would kill me if I did. I became afraid of him at that very moment. Our relationship has never been the same.

Presently, my heart will not let me visit him for birthdays or holidays. I would always say that I would go visit, but I never showed up. I forgave him for hurting me (at least I think I did) …for hurting our relationship…for throwing my trust as far as anyone could see it. When this memory comes to mind, I think of Jesus on the Cross when He speaks of the thieves on the crosses next to Him. He says, "Forgive them Father, for they know not what they do." And I believe to this day, that he did not have God in his life. This would not have happened if he had an ounce of God's love, grace, and mercy in his body. His job was to protect me…not hurt and destroy me.

The sexual assault did not stop there. There were two uncles and a cousin that thought that it was okay to continue with this "trend." I kept silent…kept my mouth closed. I cried a lot of days and nights. I thought that this family secret was not to be shared with anybody. I could get in trouble, and I didn't want that. I didn't want confusion…I didn't want seclusion…I didn't want attitude. I wanted to "keep the peace." So I kept silent. Not knowing that this act would follow me all the days of my life.

Eventually, the abuse stopped happening physically, but it left me mentally disabled. I was so distraught toward the male species that I blamed them all for what only four men did to me when I was just a kid. I blamed everyone…even me. How could I let something like this happen??

I continued on through the years just getting by…clubbing, drinking, being promiscuous, and barely working. I had two children by the age of 21, and I was a high school graduate. But I wasn't fulfilled. I felt empty. Ignoring all of God's signs, I kept clubbing, drinking, and being promiscuous, and I got absolutely nowhere. I witnessed my younger sisters get Bachelors and Masters degrees and here I was, almost forty years old and just getting an Associate's in Business Administration.

By this time in my life, I had begun to talk with Momma about things going on in my life and she used her experience to help me get through some tough times. After self-examining and realizing the things I am capable of, I stopped blaming myself.

Today, I am learning to let go of things that are not productive in helping me learn my purpose and reach my destiny. I recite positive affirmations that help me realize that, "I am worthy of everything that God has for me," "I am fearfully and wonderfully made," "God cares for me," and "He will give me the desires of my heart." And I trust that God will heal me whole-heartedly…mind, body, and soul. I pray that God forgives those four men for what they have done to me and many others. With a gracious and merciful God and my beautiful, supportive family, I am sure to find Peace after Pain…

Resa

Reflections from Momma

My oldest daughter, Teresa

I am very proud of ALL OF MY CHILDREN. They are what kept me going and striving for betterment. My children were my heart. Always were, always will be. I loved them all the same. Although I had a so-called husband, I always felt like a single parent. It was my job to provide for them. I sometimes worked two jobs to make ends meet.

My oldest had a baby fresh out of high school. She moved to Memphis, Tennessee to live with my aunt to go to school, because I could not afford the commute from Clarksdale, Mississippi everyday. She would come home on Friday and return to Memphis on Sunday evening. I kept the baby all week, even while I worked, because I wanted her to complete her studies in the medical profession.

After all the long nights with her baby and countless dollars, she did not complete the course. She let a man sway her away from her dreams and potential of becoming a Medical Assistant. Since that time, she had been in and out of low-paying jobs.

I continue to pray for her and ask God to show her the way. He used her sisters to show her what she was losing out on by not using her gifts God gave her. She finally opened up as to why she was afraid to strive for better. She had always been afraid of rejection. She didn't apply for high-paying jobs because she didn't want to hear the words "No".

Once she came out of her shell and applied, she got the job! Her soul is at peace because now she can provide for her family. I am giving God the glory everyday! I am so proud of her. My prayers have been answered. Thank you Jesus!

"Our deepest fear is not that we are inadequate. Our deepest fear is that we are powerful beyond measure. It is our light, not our darkness that most frightens us. We ask ourselves, Who am I to be brilliant, gorgeous, talented, and fabulous? Actually, who are you not to be? You are a child of God. Your playing small does not serve the world." Marianne Williamson

Chapter Three

Jai is on the far right.

Jamie Y. Hopkins (formally Timmons)

#theVoice
A New Normal

I've been on this emotional healing journey for quite some time, since my late 20's to be exact, and I am now 40 years old! It's an every day battle to remain in a space of healing. A fight to never return to that dark place ever again. There's nothing there in that dark place but hopelessness, suicidal thoughts, despair, helplessness, depression, anger, bitterness, brokenness, etc. But how did I get there in the first place, you ask? Well, now that's a long story, but I'll try to make it short!

My childhood was pretty normal. I mean, everything that happened I thought was "normal". It wasn't until my late 20's that I realized just how f*$ked up it really was!!!

I was introduced to the world of perversion early on in life. I would say I had to have been around five years old. We had cousins that visited our small town from another state every now and again. The oldest male cousin would lock me in the closet with him where he would lift my skirt or pull my shorts down and play with my private parts. I never fought back because I just thought it was all a game. We were playing hide and go seek. He always found me. In the closet.

The neighborhood kids were just as perverted. I thought all kids were curious and played with one another. My neighbor, who was around my same age, said he liked me. So he would always force me into his room, or in some secluded area, pulled his little thing out and played with me with it. I don't ever remember kissing any of these boys. Just being played with. A lot. Again, I just thought it was a game. Hide and go seek took on a whole new meaning to me.

Oh and don't let me forget the ultimate game with my uncle. He was a mean man but he was never mean to me. He was mean to my aunt though. He beat the hell out of her every chance he got. But what he did to me, my mind blocked out until my late 20's.

He would force me and my cousins to watch porn. One particular movie was called something chocolate. I was too young to read so the only word that sticks out in my memory bank is chocolate on the TV screen. Anyway, the woman on the TV was having sex with two men at the same time. I remember very vividly seeing the men's private parts entering her in the front and back at the same time. And she's lying there with her legs open moaning loudly. She looked like she enjoyed it. Then she would get on her knees and put their private parts in her mouth, one at a time. Until white stuff came out of the men. They were so nasty! As a matter of fact, I remember feeling nasty while watching the movie.

My uncle would force me to emulate what I saw on the screen with my cousins, and then eventually with him. I remember a video camera in the room. I remember my aunt holding the camera. I remember his scent. I remember his body, how muscular he was, his stomach was ripped with a six pack. He was in good shape. Very strong. And very aggressive. For some reason, I remember being face-down a lot. One look that is burned in my brain is the look on my baby cousin's face as she sat by watching my uncle handle me like he handled her. The look of "I'm so sorry" on her face as she sat helpless to the side. She knew her turn was coming up soon, again.

Incest. That's the word for what he did to me between the ages of five through nine — four years consistently. But at that time, I thought it was "normal". Every kid played games like that with family members, right? That's what I thought. Did it hurt? I can't remember feeling hurt. I conditioned my mind at that age to accept it. I thought it was "normal". I guess you can say that's when my creative skill began to develop. I would force my mind to go into it's "happy place" every single time this "normal" thing would happen. I didn't realize until my late 20's just how warped my thinking was when it came to normalcy. I was being turned into a perverted individual (against my will) and didn't even know it.

My teen years weren't any better. My mom married the spawn of Satan! He hated me and my sisters. He was her second husband and the father of my baby sister. Oh how I hated that man! He would walk in the room and my stomach would literally turn and I became nauseous. I would get sick at the very sight of him. Why? Because of how he treated my mother and her children. He was only good to his daughter, who was just an infant at the time. And his family would be just as disrespectful to us, all except one who is now my mother's best friend!

Anyways, this man was an angry drunk. I remember in the beginning of his abuse, he would come home on the weekends, drunk as usual, forced my mother in the car with him and drove off into who knows where. When they returned, my mother's face was bloody. He took her somewhere to beat the hell out of her. Who knows what fed his anger. He was just always angry about something and inebriated to the max. And he took his anger out on my mother. And us kids.

The angry rants magnified with time and he began to beat her in front of us. My mother would always call my name, a sound I hear today in my head. Another memory burned in my brain. And whenever she called me, the next to the oldest of all of my sisters and also the smallest in physique, I jumped out of bed and ran to her rescue. As a teenager, I had no fear of this man. I never really cared if I could beat him or not. All I wanted him to do was to leave my mother alone. So he would turn and hit me. And I was okay with that as long as he wasn't hitting my mother. I guess you can say that's when my heart became cold, hard and angry against men.

Remember, this was my "normal". This was how my brain was conditioned at an early age. I believed every man beat his wife because that was all I saw. I believed every man drank profusely and took out his anger on his family. A family that had no violence in the home only existed on TV…. on those soap operas that my grandmother watched religiously. I learned early on that what I saw on TV was not real. This, what I went through and lived every day, THAT was real. And it sucked. And there was no way out. No help. No way to escape. Just how it was and how it would always be.

You may wonder, "Where were the cops?" We called the cops a lot. They would come, try to diffuse the situation and calm everybody down. Then say it's a domestic dispute so there is nothing they could do because my mother was married to the monster. They walked away. Even with my mother's bloody face and bruised body, they walked away. Even with that angry drunk parading around the house knowing he got away with his violent behavior, they walked away. With my faith in the justice system, or the lack thereof, they walked away. Every. Single. Time. Telling us not to provoke the angry drunk. Blaming the victim for being victimized. They walked away.

When I was 17 years old, my mom approached me with a U.S. Navy brochure. She said I should join. I didn't argue, I saw that as my opportunity to make money and get my family the hell out of that town and away from those abusive men! Except I never went back. I ran as far and as fast away as I possibly could. But you should know and be very clear that just because you left a bad situation doesn't mean that bad situation left you! My heart and my spirit was broken, and wherever I went, I took that brokenness with me.

I became extremely promiscuous and cold-hearted towards men. I didn't give a damn about their feelings. I was taught at an early age to not give a damn about men because they certainly didn't give a damn about me! So to hell with men... I will hurt you (men) before you hurt me. What a horrible way to live but I had no idea how crazy, warped, disjointed, discombobulated, and dis-eased I really was as a result of my childhood.

So here I am a young 17-year-old girl in the military, away from everything familiar, and in this whole new world. By that time, I had been sexually molested by my cousin, neighbors and uncle. I had been raped by my first date in high school. I physically battled my then step-dad my entire senior year in high school. My whole life had been fighting men since I was five years old. But now, I am in the military—an institution that trains you how to fight strategically. Imagine that.

I am independent! I have my own money, my own car and my own life. But what the hell do I do now? I knew I was smart, but I didn't know that I was broken. So subconsciously I set out to seek vengeance on all of these evil men! Not the ones in my family, but the ones that tried to be in a relationship with me. I would immediately tell them that all I wanted was sex. And what man wouldn't want that? I was in the military! It was filled with young promiscuous kids!

I remember sleeping with a whole section of men in the barracks (a place where the soldiers slept). Not at one time! But over a period of time while I was in military school, studying to become an Intelligence Specialist. Matter of fact, it became a game to me. I only slept with men and their friends. It was a prerequisite, if you will. Because really, I just wanted to "play" them just like they played women. (Remember my mind was warped and I was in complete dysfunction.)

I became known in the barracks as the easy one. And boy did they flock to me! I didn't want a relationship and I never called them afterwards. They only got one shot with me so make it good. Or else I would blast your a$$ all over campus how you sucked in bed! I tore down reputations and relationships left and right. Dare to enter my path of destruction if you will. Can I add that I never used protection?

So let's dig into that for a little. I never used a condom, didn't take birth control pills, wasn't concerned about AIDS or any other sexually transmitted diseases. You know why? Because I didn't give a damn if I lived or died. I didn't love myself enough to care. Hell, the way I thought about it, if I died, I would finally be free.

But what was I running from? I was running from the nightmares. I was running from my upbringing. I was running from my crushed dreams and aspirations. I was running from that little girl inside of me that kept crying all the damn time! She worked my nerves really badly! Won't she just shut the hell up??? Running.

Well, the inevitable happened. I got pregnant. It was at the end of my tour of intelligence school and I was getting ready to be stationed in Japan. So here I am, seventeen and pregnant by a man I hardly knew and didn't even like for real! I would love to say that getting pregnant changed my behavior, but it didn't. It just took it to a whole new level. I've always been good at adjusting.

I couldn't be pregnant and on a military ship, so the military sent me to San Diego, California. There, I continued my promiscuous behavior, even while pregnant. Except, that time, I was looking for a baby daddy. I settled down with two men, both friends, and neither knew about the other. That shocked me that I was able to play them as long as I did because apparently they never talked about me to each other.

Life was good (so I thought). I had settled down with two men and all I really had to do was juggle when I spent time with them. We were all in the military on the same base and lived in the same barracks. I was proud that I was able to carry on this game during my whole pregnancy and even after I gave birth.

Though no matter how much I hated men outwardly, inwardly I really desired more than anything to be loved. Not realizing that I didn't love myself, I kept secretly seeking love from others, especially men. Confusing right? Neglect, abandonment, abuse…those were my normal realities, but I wanted so badly to change that; I just didn't know how. So I continued with the games. The lying, the cheating, the tearing down games with men… it was so out of control.

Then I met the man that I would marry. I don't know what it was about him, but he was the first man that I fell head over heels in love with. The problem was, he had a fiancé that lived in Oakland, California. That didn't stop me from pursuing him though. And it didn't stop him from sleeping with me. You see, my weapon was between my legs. Guess who taught me that? That's right, my damn uncle.

No wonder our relationship never really worked out. It started on a pretense of lies and spawned into more lies and deceit. That will be a whole other book in and of itself! I trusted no man. Period.

But it was this man, after we married, that said the magical words to me that changed my life forever! He said to me at the breakfast table, "I am not your uncle."

At that very moment, I realized just how f*$&@d up I was! My past haunted me. It was the reason I was the way I was. Why I was so depressed. Why I was so unhappy. Why I was so lonely even though I had a husband and four children (one biological and three step children). I hated life because I felt like life hated me. Those words stung deeply but opened my eyes to finally accepting the fact that I needed professional help. This monster was bigger than I thought and bigger than I (or my husband) could handle.

We eventually divorced, but that was when my healing journey really began! I changed my mission of killing every soul of a man to seeking peace and healing for myself. I began to pursue my new "normal". Not the normal that I was raised with, but the normal that I currently live today. I made a decision. I took a chance. I returned to my first love: God.

You see, I was raised in the church. My mother made sure every Sunday we were dropped off at church. My grandmothers were there every Sunday, serving on the usher board and making sure we behaved during service. I loved singing in the choir. I loved Bible Vacation school for the kids during the summer. I loved volunteering at the local food shelter, fixing plates for the homeless. These are the memories God brought back to me - the times when I felt at peace and happy.

Pastor Black, may his soul rest in peace, would sing this one song every Sunday: *Without God, I could do nothing. Without Him, I would fail. Without Him, my life would be rugged like a ship without a sail.*

He sang this song every single Sunday to the point when us kids would know when to cue the music! We expected to hear this song at the same time in every service. As a kid, I didn't understand the words. But today, at the age of 40, when I get into a place of total weakness and despair, guess what song comes to my spirit? *Without God, I could do nothing. Without Him, I would fail. Without Him, my life would be rugged like a ship without a sail.*

Every single thing I have gone through in my entire life has not been in vain. God took all of my broken pieces, my warped sense of reality, my mistakes and bad choices, my anger and spiteful intentions… Truth be told, He kept me all of those wild, promiscuous years when I cared about no one and nothing. He saved me from sexually transmitted diseases. He saved me from life-threatening diseases. He saved me and He took all of those broken pieces and put me back together. He healed my broken heart. He soothed my aching pain. He created in me a new heart rid of unforgiveness and anger. I am whole because I made a decision to let it all go.

I had to let go of my past. Let go of my disappointments. Let go of all of the bad choices I've made. Forgive myself and forgive others. And then, open my heart to true love.

When I stopped looking for love, love found me. A man that was created for the depths of my soul. A man that was created to be my provider and protector. And I was created to be his healer. To comfort and mend his broken heart. To be to him what God is to me. And together, we are one. One with God and one with each other.

The moral of my story is there is life after death. The moment YOU choose life. *My past does not define me, it refines me.*

Jai

Reflections from Momma

My second oldest daughter, Jamie

What can I say? She has always been a "small" loud mouth and hot head. You know the saying, "the littlest is always the loudest and feistiest." TRUE!! That's her. She was the bossiest of all. Trying to tell the older ones what to do. She was destined for success from day one.

She had a newspaper delivery job as a teenager. Not happy with the job because it didn't pay what she thought it should have. So after graduating from high school, she went off to college. After only a year, maybe it was just a semester, she decided to join the military. That was one of my saddest days to have my baby leave home. Not knowing whether she would come home again. But she put her whole heart into it and succeeded.

She had some let downs, rejection and hurdles during her life. Sometimes I know she felt like life threw her a hard ball. Although she had a husband and daughter, she felt all alone many days and nights. When you have to fall asleep with tears in your eyes, depression is not far away. They say communication is the best medicine. But how if you don't trust the person you're talking to to understand what you are feeling and why. Most times, communication is listening. Therapists often say people who are dealing with situations just need an open ear.

With the help of the good Lord, continuous prayer, family and friends, she is learning how to deal with her pain. The first step is to admit it to yourself. The Lord has removed obstacles and people out of her OLD life to bring her to the NEW life that was destined for her since before she was born. I couldn't be more proud of her at this very moment. She is striving for excellence. She has opened up her heart to feel the love that she has always wanted and deserved.

I always tell her to let God take control and He will show you the way, when you don't see it. When you stop trying to fix things beyond your control. She has been an inspiration and role model for her sisters. Her accomplishment has made them want to strive harder to accept life hurdles and move forward with dignity and grace.

"We must embrace pain and burn it as fuel for our journey." Kenji Miyazawa

Chapter Four

Trina is in the middle.

Katrina M. Brown

#theEncourager
Afraid of the Dark

September 1979, a beautiful five pound baby girl was born. Oh, I'm sorry, that beautiful girl is me, Katrina! Who knew that someone so little, fragile, innocent, and precious would soon face a dramatic life change?

My life as a child should have been fun, stress free, and no worries. Well, it wasn't. At some point, my mom met Titus. I'm not sure at what age, but I had to have been young since I thought he was my father because I grew up around him.

My childhood should have been a happy one, but it wasn't. My childhood was taken away by a man who I thought was my father. Yes, by Titus. Around the age of two or three, Titus started molesting me. I was afraid, scared, confused, in pain and couldn't understand how a person who loves you so much could hurt you so bad.

I can remember him saying, "Don't tell mommy. This is between me and you because daddy loves you." Every night, when the light went out, I could feel his presence coming into my room, getting in my bed, and taking my panties off. He would play around between my legs, take my feet and roll his manhood between them. Then he would take his manhood and put it between my legs.

Oh how it hurt so bad! I was crying for my mom and he would tell me to be quiet. I cried out for my mom but I'm not sure if she even heard me, or if she knew what he was doing. I was so afraid of him because he was very abusive. On several occasions when I was left alone with him, he made me watch naked people on TV with him. Titus was a very sick man. There were plenty of times I went in their room and naked people were on the TV. When I got much older I found out the naked people on the TV were actually porn.

Titus molested me over and over. He would even give me a bath. I can remember him washing between my legs and it hurt badly. Titus molesting me became part of what I expected. I never told anyone.

Did my mom know? She was home most of the time when it happened. I was her little girl. Why didn't she protect me? Was she afraid of what Titus might do to her? Titus abused my mom also. He used to beat her up on several occasions. One time I can remember us running away and being at my grandmother's house, but we ended up going back. Once again, the house was dark.

It's nighttime and Titus comes into my room. He once again takes his manhood and put it between my legs. *Make it stop! Don't hurt me daddy! Daddy it hurts! Save me mommy!* All of this was going through my mind.

Some way, somehow the truth came out about what Titus was doing, and I was taken out of that home and eventually went to live with my aunt and cousins, also known as my new mom and sisters. As I got older, I found out Titus was not my dad, he was my step-father. That still didn't make me feel better because he should have treated me like I was his own. You don't hurt those you love. Maybe he didn't love me or maybe the sickness he had in his mind dominated him.

Anyway, I thank my aunt for saving me from Titus, but the damage was already done. I was taken away from a woman who carried me for nine months, nurtured me while I was in her womb, knew my heart beat and protected me while I was in her belly. She didn't get the chance to raise her only beautiful baby girl because of Titus. I never even got the chance to have that bond a mother and daughter should, and are suppose, to have.

Well, I was away from Titus, so I guess that's a start. Living with my aunt and cousins was okay. I love them dearly and wouldn't replace them for nothing in the world. So, I know you're thinking life for me was great at that point…NO! No one ever sat me down and explained to me what happened to me or why I was taken from my mom.

I don't remember getting counseling either for the abuse. All I know is I had nightmares all the time about what happened. Being molested haunted me the majority of my life. I was afraid of the dark because this was the time all bad things happened. I was also afraid to be around men because I thought they would hurt me too.

Since it turned out Titus was my step-father, I wanted to know who my real father was and all I got from my own family was the run around. It seemed like my life was a secret which made me confused about who I really was. Well, life was going okay for us until my aunt met Jimmy.

Jimmy was a wolf in sheep's clothing. My cousins and I didn't like him from the start, but we were kids, so there was nothing we could do. At their wedding we cried because even though we were children, we knew it was a mistake. Well, the wolf was ready to attack. We watched Jimmy abuse my aunt constantly. Sometimes he abused us mentally. A couple of times I watched him abuse my cousins physically.

Jimmy had a daughter by my aunt and that was his prize possession. She got whatever she wanted. A blind person could see she was treated differently than us. She was Jimmy's seed, so no harm would come to her. The abuse towards the rest of us just became worse and worse. There were even rumors that he was cheating on my aunt.

Okay, I'm a teenager now and I'm fed up with all of this abuse and pain. It had to stop. See, we were raised in the church and taught about God at an early age. We went to church every Sunday. I loved church. It made me feel all giddy and warm inside. I especially loved to hear the choir sing. They sounded like angels. It gave me a sense of peace to escape all the pain I was feeling. Going to church and having faith in God was how we were able to make it in life.

Although I was raised in church, I sometimes wondered how God could allow children to go through things like I did, but I later learned that God has a plan and a purpose for our lives even when we don't understand. Though I was confused, afraid, and had no sense of direction, all I wanted to know was what could I do to save my family. Well, I could kill Jimmy and everything would be okay. So I started plotting how I was going to kill Jimmy and get him out of our lives. The closer I got to doing it, I thought about it—If I kill Jimmy, I would be taken away from my cousins and aunt. I didn't want that to happen because I loved them too much and they were a part of me, and I was a part of them.

So I did the only thing I could do to escape the pain—I ran away. Now this was not a good plan either because I allowed a man, who was old enough to be my dad, persuade me that he would stop the pain. Well guess what, he didn't stop the pain. He created more. The police eventually found me, but I was so messed up in the mind that I moved back in with the man. I know what you're thinking, "How could you?" Well, this was the only life I knew. I grew up this way.

The very thing I wanted to escape from happened to me. I was abused sexually, mentally and physically. I lost all consciousness of who I was. One day, my cousins came to visit me. I was so happy to see them. I wanted to go home with them, but I was too afraid of "Mister". He threatened to kill me if I ever tried to leave and I believed him because he choked me out several times.

I never knew if I was going to wake up, but I did. I was very afraid of him! Have you ever had someone to put a gun in your private and tell you they would blow it off? Yes, this happened to me. You can imagine how scared I was. Ironically, he had a picture of what God was supposed to look like on his bathroom wall. I prayed to this picture everyday to let me get home. That was the only thing I knew to do… pray.

One day, I built up the courage to call my grandma, and she and my uncle came to take me home. What a relief! Now that I lived with my grandma, life got better for me. I didn't have to worry about the abuse anymore. I guess it is safe to say that I wasn't making sound judgments. How could I? I had no clue of who I was. All I knew was pain. I can barely remember being a child sometimes, because my brain has tried to block out all the bad memories and visions I kept having. See, all this pain and hurt made me confused about love. How could you hurt and abuse somebody you love? If this was love I didn't want it.

Growing up for me was hard. I allowed guys to make a fool of me because I wanted to feel accepted and not rejected. I did so much to please others that I forgot about myself. In 1996, I ended up getting pregnant and having a baby boy at 17-years-old. It was tough because I had to work, take care of him and go to school. My life seemed like it was over. Things didn't work out with my son's father. I finally graduated high school in 1998 and got a job at the casino. This is where I met someone who treated me like a queen, and accepted my son like he was his own.

We dated for two years before I became pregnant again. In the beginning, it was a happy moment. Then memories of my past molestation was coming back to haunt me. In 2001, I ended up losing my baby boy at 22 weeks of pregnancy. After premature delivery, he lived two hours and ten minutes before he died. This broke my heart. The doctor said I had an incompetent cervix which was caused by trauma. They asked if I had been hurt before and I said, "No". In the back of my mind, I knew I had been molested when I was young, but didn't want to bring up my past to the doctor.

Six months later in October 2001, after I lost my baby boy, I married my then boyfriend. Well, our lives moved on and, once again, I ended up pregnant in 2003. I know what you are thinking…that's great! Well, NO! I ended up losing a baby girl at 22 weeks. Yes, it happened again! Once again the doctor told me I had an incompetent cervix which could be caused by trauma to the cervix. This caused me to go into depression.

Why does this keep happening to me? Am I being punished? My husband was trying to comfort me, but I didn't want it. I was messed up inside. I ended up going through life like a robot. I was just existing. My marriage wasn't on the best of terms either. After I lost my baby girl, I ended up pregnant again. I showed no signs of affection and really didn't care about the pregnancy because I was going to lose this baby too. Well, God sent me an angel for a doctor. He put a cerclage in my cervix to hold my cervix closed long enough for the baby to survive.

I had a baby girl in 2004. This was real and I was happy. She was born prematurely but she made it. Then the blessings kept coming. I had a baby boy in 2005. Yes, I had another baby back-to-back, but it's okay, I'm married. Funny huh? Just a little humor to make you laugh from reading all of this sadness.

Even though I had these beautiful children, it still seemed like something was missing. I still didn't know who I was or what I wanted in life. This caused my marriage to suffer and I told my husband we needed to separate. We were separated for two years but we still communicated and raised the children together.

My birth mother came back into the picture, and she helped me with the kids. We actually ended up getting close and started doing mother-daughter things together like shopping, getting our hair done and going out to eat. We talked a little about my past, and she shared that she was afraid of Titus. I forgave her. She was my mom and I loved her. We spent three months together getting to know one another. I didn't know this time was about to be cut short.

In January 2012, my husband found my mom dead in my apartment. She had an acute heart attack. She was gone. I was hurt. I was enjoying spending time with her and getting to know her. This seemed unreal and like a dream. I just saw her that morning before I went to work.

So we laid my mom to rest and guess who came to the funeral?!! Yes, Titus. I was so depressed and sad that I felt nothing when I saw him. Maybe at that point he really did love my mom. I'm not sure. My husband was really there for me when my mom died. We ended up getting back together and getting counseling from our Pastor. We had to start dating all over again and we left what happened in the past, in the past.

Now our marriage is stronger than ever. My faith in God has increased and I'm learning how to have a closer relationship with Him. See, all my life I knew I was different and not like others, but it's okay. God's children are peculiar people. I learned the only way to get rid of the empty feeling was to let go of all the hurt, pain, and abuse I had all locked inside. You see, even though I am a grown woman on the outside, that little girl that was molested is still on the inside and needs to be set free. The only person that can free her is me. I can no longer be the power source to that abuse, and it is time for me to disconnect from it. See, I am tired of feeling empty inside and having no sense of purpose. I knew it was time to speak out about what happened because it was eating me alive inside.

In order for these chains to be broken I had to face my childhood so I could be free. I want to be free! I had to go back to the landmark. Remember, I was raised in the church, and the Spirit of God was in me, however, as a result of all of the drama I had going on in my life, I stopped going to church and lost all sense of direction and self. Nonetheless, God is so awesome that He always welcomes us back with open arms.

I knew if I was going to be free I had to go back to the One Who created me. Not my mom and dad, but God. See, He knows all about me because He is my Creator. Once I went back to church and started focusing on God, and not my circumstance,

God started renewing my mind, increasing my faith and restoring my joy.

I pray constantly to God about renewing my mind because all of the negative things that happened in my life kept playing over and over in my mind like a movie. The more I kept focusing on God and started praising and worshipping Him, the stronger and better I became.

Then one day my Pastor preached a sermon on forgiveness. "Are you serious?" is what I thought. I have to forgive Titus for molesting me? I was only a child and they were monsters. Well, if I wanted God to forgive me for my wrong doings I had to forgive people who hurt me. I could no longer give them power over me. You know, when you truly forgive someone you can look them in the eye and not feel afraid, or vengeful. That means healing is taking place.

Thank God for my family raising us in the church so we could learn about God, because that's how we all survived. We made it on broken pieces. See, it's not where you start but where you end up. I really didn't want to write this book because I didn't want anyone to know about my life. I'd been praying to God about my purpose and my destiny. I don't understand or know why I was molested but I am going to use what happened to me as a voice for those who are scared and/or ashamed to tell someone they were molested.

My story can also help those who are currently being molested. If I can save someone from committing suicide, murdering someone, or even losing their mind, then I want to do it. See, I know that I have a purpose in life and I will live it out to the fullest. I have a voice and I will be heard. I am not operating out of fear anymore. I am confident, beautiful, strong, and most importantly, I am a child of the Most High! I have power and value and no one can take that from me ever again.

Trina

Reflections from Momma

My middle daughter, Katrina

I really don't know what to say, Lord. She is a very spiritual and loving young lady. She shows a smile when deep down her heart is hurting. Only when she thinks about the goodness of God and how far He has brought her, is when the tears flow. She has been through one disaster after another. She tried to deal with each one by herself and began having anxiety attacks. God told her to give Him her troubles and He will guide her through. She trusted and believed in Him and He is doing just that.

She loves family. She gives so much of herself to others. You see the glow in her eyes when she walks in the room. But she has not come completely to terms with her past. She's afraid that people will treat her differently. She opens up to certain people. I tell her all the time, they are not going to judge you, they are trying to heal just like you. Talking about the situation is a process of healing.

"I am fantastic, I'm awesome, I'm amazing, I'm worthy, I'm emotional, I'm human, and I need to make sure he's deserving of me." Unknown

Chapter Five

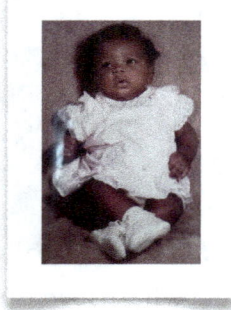 

Josie L. Hopkins

#ForeverHumble
He Loves Me, He Loves Me Not

October 16, 2001, I was preparing to begin my shift at work when I noticed him walking towards me. He was 6'2, fair skinned, bald head, immaculate smile, and smelled of sandalwood and bergamot. As he shook my hand to introduce himself, our eyes were intensely connected. We became inseparable from that day forward.

He was the perfect gentleman and, after searching for so many years, I had finally met the man of my dreams…so I thought. Unbeknownst to me, my life was about to change dramatically. Dr. Martin Luther King, Jr. had a dream, but this right here turned out to be a nightmare.

In the beginning, Ray spent every chance he could with me. As soon as he left my presence, we would talk on the phone until he arrived home. The sex was amazing, he was funny, and, of all the women he could be with, he chose me. I guess it is safe to say we were in that honeymoon phase of the relationship.

After three years of dating, Ray and I decided to move in together, along with my two young sons. Overwhelmed with excitement, the kids and I started a new life. One that I didn't think either of us were prepared for. Ray normally worked late night shifts at the casino, while I worked in the evening. This allowed us to rotate schedules with the kids being so young.

About a year into cohabiting, Ray began to change. He took his phone calls outside, stopped coming home at night, and we argued more than usual. It gave me the impression that the family life was becoming a bit exhausting for him. After all, he was only in his early 30's, which is the prime years for single men. But we never conversed about him being unhappy or the need to separate.

On November 11, 2005, Ray insisted on taking me to work. He knew how much I enjoyed the pleasure of him driving me around, especially to and from work. On a normal day, we checked in with each other to make sure the family was doing well. This particular day, something was off. I couldn't reach him or the kids all day and began to worry. Shortly before 10:00 p.m., my children walked into my workplace without Ray. Glad to see them, I questioned to see if Ray was outside waiting and he wasn't.

He left $1,000 in my son's coat pocket and left us stranded at the casino. My gracious coworker, Racheal, gave us a ride home, only to find that he wiped the apartment clean. This was the first red flag. It took months to recover from this lost, but eventually we did.

Several months of struggling to find transportation, acquiring caretakers for the boys, and so much more, resulted into us finding a home elsewhere. I was determined to find Ray because I had convinced myself that I could not make it without him. Unfortunately, once I found him, another woman was leaving his house. The determination of not being alone was overshadowed by what was just witnessed with mine own eyes. This was the second red flag.

Despite what I just saw with the woman walking out of his house, I walked in and gave him my plea for help. The stipulations of his demands were crucial, but you know what they say, beggars can't be choosey, so I went along with it. As long as we were together.

For years following, the mental, physical, verbal, and emotional abuse were astounding. There was even a moment when he dragged me in the car outside of my mother's house! After pleading for him to stop, he laughed and said, "Get your dumb ass in the car." This was the third red flag.

If I wanted "security", these were the things I had to endure — embarrassment, disrespect, and hatred. The signs were prevalent, but I chose to ignore them for comfort and love... or shall I say, *my* idea of comfort and love. The final straw erupted one morning when Ray came home from work and started a dispute. Well, this day was the wrong day for him...point, blank, period.

For once, there was a little fight left in me and I had to take a stance. How much longer do I continue to allow this man to knock me upside my head in front of my children? I was tired of it and I knew my life, and my children's lives, depended on my decision at that very moment. I became SILENT NO MORE!

Needless to say, my mother had to bail me out of jail and gave me her infamous words of wisdom as always, "You know, I never get in your business, but you have my grandkids to care for. All I am going to say, is when you are tired, you will leave." Those words saved my life! She saved me. My mother saved us. For that I am forever grateful and indebted to her.

My mother's words forced me into making my first step to admitting there was a problem. One that does not come with accounting terminology (I worked in the finance department so accounting was my profession). The next day, July 2008, I called Mom and asked that she send a car to pick us up immediately. I'd come to the conclusion that I was indeed running on fumes.

December 8, 2008, the boys and I relocated to Columbia, Maryland. This move was going to be the beginning of a fresh start, is what I tried to convince myself. But my past would not let go of me. Matter of fact, I was ready to give it all up when I seriously contemplated a decision to move back to Mississippi to marry the man that caused me so much hurt and pain. A thousand miles away from my abuser made me miss him more. Reality sat in quickly with the snap of a finger. Remembering why I moved to Maryland in the first place was enough to keep me grounded, though it was not easy. I could not get him off of my mind, but I was saved by one thing: my love for my kids. My children's best interest was, and still remains, a prominent factor in the majority of my decisions. So, despite how much I missed Ray, I stayed in Maryland.

Three attempts at intimate relationships after Ray, and, you guessed it, every last one of them were an epic fail! It seemed as if the toxic pattern was repeating itself, except for the physical abuse. Cheating, lying, verbal abuse, disrespect, mental abuse, disappointment, miscarriage, broken engagements. What was going on?

Where is it written that a woman must lower her standards to have a partner? Why is loyalty a thing of the past? How does one self-absorb any of this? I couldn't begin to fathom why it was so hard for me to be happy. *Why won't he love me? What have I done for him to treat me like this?*

The pain I had endured from these men were unspeakable. I am most humble to God, my mother, my family, and myself for being able to realize my worth and being alive to speak about it. Not many abused women live to tell their story. This has been a long healing process. A process in which I take full responsibility and appreciation.

Two years ago, I made the executive decision to seek therapy. After engaging in tumultuous relationships, there was a need to make sure that I'd dealt with the agony instead of burying it deep. I had to learn how to give myself permission to have certain feelings at any given time. However, the key to my healing was not allowing myself to become complacent in those feelings for too long. There was also a need to help my children heal from all they witnessed.

Raising two teenage boys on the road to become men was now an even harder challenge than before. I wholeheartedly blame myself. They didn't ask for it, to see it, to be involved in it, or recover from it. The abuse I encountered in the past had been a detriment to my children's mental stability. It has been expressed both verbally and emotionally, how being a witness to such abuse can trigger similar habits. It is instilled in them to not become a product of their environment, but rather set an example. They are stronger than this.

While reiterating that the first step to recovery is admitting that you have a problem, please allow me to reintroduce myself. Hi, my name is Josie and I was afraid of loving myself.

Too often, we look for love, comfort, stability, peace, and happiness in people and things that either can't reciprocate or don't know how to provide it. Secondly, in all fairness, I can't ask something of someone when I haven't done the work myself. Being afraid to love myself came from an insecurity that was embedded in my mind years ago. Since I couldn't or refused to love myself, the thought of him loving me was more than enough.

The hardest thing one must convince is the mind. Therefore, I choose not to succumb to my pain, but live life victoriously. God has kept me through it all, even within my faults. #ForeverHumble I had to surrender my all to God for Him to bless me tremendously with His love and grace. I stand firm and strong on my faith.

A special thanks to Ray for allowing me to experience the pain, hurt, and abuse firsthand. Had it not been for him, I would've never relocated and embarked on this wonderful journey. God has placed a divine calling on my life and that will not be taken for granted. It has been an honor for me to bless others with financial guidance and motivation to live a prosperous life. I live vicariously by allowing others to experience my life's message.

Last, and certainly not least, I want to give a special thanks to my new best friend, Sam. The same year I started therapy was the same year I met, Sam. He was kind, gentle, understanding, and patient… very patient! But he came in my life at a time that I was broken and hurt, so he took a lot of the backlash for my past pain. Instead of running for the hills, he stuck around. Thirteen years of buried pain that I had to work through in only two years of therapy. And Sam was right by my side every step of the way.

So again, I want to give a special thanks to Sam, my best friend. You are the epitome of what a God-fearing man resembles. You have allowed me to love you in spite of the pain and for that I am #ForeverHumble. Thank you for being patient with me, loving me in your own special way, helping me to grow, nurturing the wounds, laughing until it hurts, trusting unconditionally, walking with me as I walk in my purpose, being my prayer warrior, but most importantly, showing me that love and change can coexist.

Jo

Reflections from Momma

My next to the youngest daughter, Josie

What can I say about this child? As a teenager, she gave me some gray hairs. She was very self-centered and disobedient as a child. Whatever I told her to do, she would do the opposite. She thought her way was always right and nobody else's opinion mattered. Before completing high school, she had a baby and left home. That's when the abuse began. She had several abusive relationships. It took the sight of tears in her oldest son's eyes to realize enough was enough before she fought back. She ended up in jail, but I could not have been more proud of her for standing up for herself.

Although I was saddened when she moved out of the state with the children, I knew it was time for her to feel safe and begin the healing process.

"What's the greater risk? Letting go of what people think - or letting go of how I feel, what I believe, and who I am?" Brené Brown

Chapter Six

Sherika is on the left.

Sherika J. Shedwick

#BabyGirl
My Wake Up Call

Growing up the youngest of many girls would seem like a wonderful thing, but in actuality it's very competitive and isolating. I was the baby sister on both sides. On my mother's side, I was the youngest of five kids; and my oldest sisters had a different father. Contrary, on my father's side, I was the youngest of countless kids; and my sisters had different mothers. So my being the youngest of all of my sisters and brothers, I often felt out of place and left out. It had its ups and downs to say the least.

I am now 29 years old with three wonderful kids. Not every journey in life was handled with a silver or golden spoon (meaning it didn't come easy to me), but I learned so many lessons with every obstacle coming up in this corrupted world.

I've heard most of my life, particularly from my sisters, that I am a spoiled brat. They seemed to think that I get everything I want, and perhaps that was true as a kid. My dad bought me a lot of candy and snacks as a kid. But what my sisters didn't understand at that time, was that I felt so alone. Even with all of them, I felt like they really didn't know who I was, or bothered to get to know me. Many times, I hurt because of that. But I was just a kid. So I had to figure it out on my own.

What most people called "spoiled", I called it adapting to what I learned in *society* in order to fit in and survive. My lessons came from outside of my home, partly. This way of upbringing and adaptation led me to think and feel the way I do about a lot of things: my perceptions on life, the way my heart responds, the way I see myself through my own lens… but through this journey of finding my way, it all boiled down to my story: "Loving yourself before loving someone else".

Truth be told, my father never really taught me how a man should love a woman. I mean, what he taught me was unhealthy and not the true meaning of love. You've read my sisters stories in this book, you know exactly why I say that. What they endured was at the hands of my father. So what he taught me about how to be a man and how to love your woman is partly the reason why I went through what I went through in my own relationships.

A simple lesson he could've shown me was how to vet out the good from the bad boys I was dating. How I was supposed to bring them home to meet my parents, and let them question him before taking out "baby girl", etc. Like, show me that I matter to you enough to care about who I was being intimate with! Instead, I jumped into this cruel world without a clue on how to respond to peer pressure, how to feel when given the simplest compliment or just say 'thank you' and keep it moving… I yearned for those compliments my dad never gave me. I yearned for that attention he neglected to fulfill in his baby girl's life. So I searched for it elsewhere. And what I found terrorized my soul!

Being the juicy short bubbly young lady that always smiled, I accepted all compliments from males; and gifts made things so much better! Oh, I was in love then. I was a sucker for love. Any man that gave me the attention a girl needed, said the right things and did the right things, had my heart. I was in love. Then along came Gino.

Little did I know when I first met Gino, that not only didn't he know what love was, but he damn sure didn't know how to love, respect, or appreciate a woman like myself. Many years of friendship turned into a romantic relationship, that later included the birth of a child. But to make the "situation-ship" even worse, I endured and allowed everything that was offered with this connection. When you fall in love with someone like this man, there's no "getting out"… it was like he was the devil in disguise.

I love God with all of my being because I was raised in church. My mother and grandmother made sure that we attended every church service, Vacation Bible School, and such. So I grew up with a love for God in my heart, but loving Gino was addictive. He was like my drug, I needed him at night to sleep. I needed him to help me make decisions on everything; I mean, if he wasn't included in every part of my life, I felt incomplete.

Gino had his ways of getting things out of me whether I had it or not. If I didn't have the money, I would find it somehow. I always found a way to get things done to please my man. I was dead on the inside when it came to Gino. I didn't matter. What I wanted didn't matter. All that mattered was getting Gino's approval and making him happy. Though it took me forever to wake up from Gino's curse, it only took one cold night to wake up from the 'dead'. It was either wake up or be killed. I'll tell you about that night in a few.

Plenty of times God would show me which path He wanted me to take, but I always chose another route because somewhere on my route I knew I would meet up with Him again. Little did I know that taking my route would almost cost me my life! Had I listened then to what I know now, I perhaps could've saved myself a lot of heartache and pain. But no one understood just how much I needed Gino. What I really needed was a man to love me. ME… the girl who everyone ignored and neglected and pushed aside. The girl who felt all alone and abandoned. The girl who no one really saw. But Gino.

Though Gino and I had our ups and downs, break ups and make ups, he always came back. And every time he came back, he was nice. We had great conversations. We hung out for a little while and things were going great again, which made me miss everything we once had. I was back under his curse. Just like that.

Things were always good for a little while and then it happened again… it was a vicious cycle. That wake up call that either I get it together or I die. This last time though, on that one cold night, I was awakened out of my dream on what I thought was love. I was awakened to the fact that in reality, I was never taught how a man should love a woman.

So many bad memories of this toxic relationship with Gino, I just try to drown them in my soul, praying they never afloat. Being abused mentally and emotionally, in my opinion, never compared to this physical abuse I endured during this situationship. I know now that it was never a real relationship. This man treated me like I was inhumane. I'd been slapped, kicked, called useless and worthless, called a bad parent, good for nothing; but through it all, I always forgave him with a simple, "I'm sorry, I love you." "Don't leave me, you're all I have." "I'll never do it again." Gino knew exactly what to say to get me to stay with him. And I did.

Now the moment I've been talking about my wake up call. That one cold night. This is not easy to share, but I am ready to share it now FINALLY:

Coming home from a party, thinking everything was okay, turned out to be the worst nightmare from hell. When I walked in the house, I was brutally attacked by that one man I loved more than life itself. Punch after punch, going in and out of consciousness, couldn't see for the blood running down my face over my eyes, screaming and pleading for my life, begging Gino to stop hitting me. Constantly screaming for God, at the same time telling Gino how much I loved him, bargaining with him, but the punches never stopped.

I thought maybe if I told him I loved him, he would snap out of it and stop hitting me. It didn't work. He was furious and in a rage, and my body took the blows.

Gino had no care in the world that his child was in the house too. At the end of the day, all I could think about was what this abusive relationship was doing to me. I thought he loved me but that night made me realize that he couldn't possibly love me; not the way I deserved to be loved and definitely not the way God loves me.

I had to come to the realization that I had to love myself first. I had to realize that I am an amazing and virtuous woman, because God said so. I went back to my roots of what I was taught in church. Love doesn't hurt; it doesn't make you feel less than; and it definitely does not make you put a man (especially one that means you no good) before anything that's important, especially God.

So as I go day by day thinking back on my past, I realize I allowed this to happen to myself. I'm not ashamed because this lesson should have been taught to me when I was a child. I should have learned from watching my own parents go through a tumultuous relationship; or watching my sisters and other family members go through their tumultuous relationships. I should've known better.

Now it is up to me, as an adult with my own children, to teach them to make better decisions than I did. Teaching them about lessons learned from my past as well as what is really out here in this world waiting for them to step into. Am I scared? Perhaps I was at some point!! But now I am a survivor because I am here today to tell my story.

Please understand this is NOT ALL OF IT, but the most important message I want to share is this: You can't love anyone else until you learn to love yourself first.

After years of physical, emotional and verbal abuse, I am glad to say that at 29-years-old, I've finally learned how to love myself from within before I try to love the outside nature AGAIN. I thank God for every lesson I've learned, and still learning, in life; every path I walked down and will continue to walk. I just thank God for everything because without Him I would probably be dead.

Staying in an abusive relationship will only eventually end up in death. Even if you leave, you still have the emotional damage to recover from. Take a lesson from my life, realize that you are worth it and you deserve better. Love doesn't hurt. This is my story.

Johnelle

Reflections from Momma

My youngest daughter, Sherika

What can I say, she is spoiled! But I am mostly to blame. Since she was little, she has always felt like an outsider because of who her father was. There had been times when I noticed her other sisters treated her differently, like a *step*-sister rather than a real sister.

I tried to show her more affection to offset that feeling. As she grew older, she demanded more of my attention, especially when all of her sisters were in the same room. I think because of my history with men, any man that smiled at her, she was in love. She had three children by three different men, whom she has had to struggle to provide for by herself (with no help from the fathers).

The one thing that I am most proud of my youngest daughter is that she is a go-getter. She believes in providing for her children by any means necessary. As such, she works two jobs. One thing she inherited from me is her love for her children and God, and this gave her the strength and motivation to overcome all the abuse she endured.

"The strongest actions for a woman is to love herself, be herself and shine amongst those who never believed she could." Unknown

Chapter Seven

Vanessa D. Fryer

#SimplyMisUnderstood
No One Knows

    Growing up I got trapped in fairy tale land about how life was supposed to be. I think all the kid stories about a prince charming saving me and living happily ever after destroyed me mentally. As I grew older I began searching for that "fairy tale love", only to find pain, heartaches, and headaches.

    When I was about the tender age of five, I was molested by a friend's uncle. Nobody really knew about this because I never told anyone until I was sixteen years old. I remember the incident just like it happened yesterday. I went outside to play with my friends, at this time I lived in an apartment complex with my mother. I went over to their apartment and this day their mom was gone and their uncle was babysitting them. Like any other day, I assumed it was going to be normal, you know, play dolls with my friends and then go home.

This day when we were getting ready to leave out of the house, their uncle made me stay inside and sent my friends out. He told them I would be out shortly, he just needed to talk to me. I watched as he put the hook on the screen door to lock it, then walked me to the back bedroom on the right side of the hallway. At the age of five I was clueless to what was about to happen to me. He started to untie my colorful striped romper saying, "Don't tell anyone about the game we are going to play." I stood there in silence because I was confused. He then pulled down my undies and turned me around and bent me over the bed. I could hear him unzipping his pants and I turned back around facing him only to see his two toned discolored penis. I thought he got burnt or something.

He immediately turned me back around, bent me over, told me to relax, and molested me. After he had taken away my innocence, he pulled my undies back up, tied my romper back together and walked me to the front and let me out. I went home straight to the bathroom, undressed to look at my behind in the mirror to see if my butt was discolored like his penis. In my mind, I thought that his discolored burnt penis was going to make me the same way.

Now I know that I was looking at a circumcised penis. Somehow I knew that what he did wasn't right and in that moment of him taking from me which was precious I knew I would never be the same. The very next day he sent my friends over to my apartment to come and get me. I told them I couldn't come outside to play. My mother overheard me telling my friends that I couldn't come out to play and she asked me why I didn't want to go over to their house. I told her I didn't feel good and I wanted to lie down.

Eleven years later she would finally find out why I didn't want to go out to play with my friends that day. I guess being silent about what happened caused me to become angry.

Anyone that knows me knows that I will help anybody. My biggest problem was trying to please people. The only thing I ever wanted was to be appreciated, but the only thing that I received was people saying to me, "You are just like your daddy's side of the family… angry and ready to fight."

What they didn't know was that I was screaming for love and attention. I needed it and I felt like nobody was there to give it to me. My mom worked all the time and we really never had the time or the finances to do anything together. I longed for family time and I would get in my feelings when I used to see my friends going on vacations or just spending time together with their mom and dad.

To be honest, I felt like the black sheep in the family. This was one of the main reasons I was a teenage mom because I was looking for someone to make me feel like I was somebody and that I wasn't a disappointment. The enemy had me right where he wanted me because I was confused and on the road to destruction.

My son's father and I were together for about five years. I thought we were going to get married and be a family, but I was wrong. He was my first love and I was engulfed in the infamous "puppy love", or shall I say *lust*. We tried to make it work but we were both young and he didn't want to let go of the streets, or the weed, so I had to go. After the breakup with him I was hurt because we were supposed to get married, but it didn't happen and now I was stuck raising our son on my own. A single mom.

Thank God for my mom because even though she said she wasn't going to help me with my son, she and my Granny did. During this time after my breakup with my son's father, I became a party animal. I was club hopping, drinking, smoked a little weed and still managed to graduate… by the grace of God! It was a wild time for me for sure.

In the mist of me club hopping and partying all the time, I met my daughter's father. My son was four years old when he and I started our relationship. We connected instantly sexually, I think that was the only thing that kept us together after the second year. He was very abusive, more emotional than physical, but we did have our fair share of fights. A lot of our problems came because he had issues from his childhood from which he never got help or healing.

We were together six and half years. It started out all peaches and cream but hell did break out in the mist of our relationship. He told me that he cheated on me and had a daughter and a son on the way. I was okay with it because at least he was being honest with me. What he failed to mention was that he was already in a relationship prior to even meeting me. I found out about the other woman months later.

Everybody knew I was head over heels crazy about him. He knew what to do or say to make me feel just really good about myself, but with that same mouth the goodness came out of so did the destruction. If this man told me to jump I was like how high. Whatever he asked of me I did or tried my best to make it happen. Our biggest problem was he was a cheater. I mean women were calling the phone and when I answered they would hang up.

When I started working at the casino I was on graveyard shift and boy was that not a good shift to have with a man! I can remember one particular incident when I got off work early one morning and made it home only to find out he wasn't there. I went to my mom's house thinking he was there and, guess what, he wasn't. I checked the cars that were parked in my mom's yard just to make sure he wasn't in one of them and he wasn't. My thinking was that he must've gotten drunk and passed out in one of the cars in the yard. Wrong!!

I stayed at my mother's house in the kitchen sitting there waiting for him to come in and I drifted off to sleep. I woke up and it was 5:30 a.m. and still no him. I got my things to leave and go home only to make it to my car and I heard him call my name. Here he is getting out one of the cars that I checked earlier in the yard saying he got drunk and fell asleep in the car. Of course I knew he was lying and we broke up for a brief moment, and then we were back together. Now he cheated on me several times, and all the times that he cheated I took him back. It was a vicious cycle. A dysfunctional relationship at its best. But I loved him.

When he accused me of cheating on him (but never had real proof), he threatened that he was going to really hurt me. I must say he didn't fail on his threat because he literally made me lose my f@$king mind. My woman's intuition pointed me in the direction of the pain I was about to endure but never could I imagine that this person would do this to me. I was wrong again. My daughter's father ended up sleeping with my son's cousin. Matter of fact, they are still in a relationship today. Talk about load the gun and pull the trigger! Now she and I were not best of friends but we were communicable because both our sons are really close to with each other. This took a whole lot to get over because he was trying to explain that it wasn't like they just started going together, it just happened. I got one word for that… BULLSHIT!!!!!!

He won. He executed his plan and he destroyed me. On the outside I was normal but on the inside I was dying. Let's not leave out that even though he left me because he assumed I was cheating and that he was stressing how happy he was there, we were still having sex. I think I did that out of spite though. I wanted to hurt them both but I finally figured out that I was only hurting myself. I was still emotionally attached to this man. After all that he put me through, I still loved him.

That soul tie was deep. I must admit that for about a week after the break-up, I kept my daughter from him; but when I realized it was going to do more damage than good, I started to let her go back to their house so he could be a part of her life. Now during this process he continued to try to destroy me as a person by telling people that I wasn't a good mother but the woman he dated was a better mother to my daughter than me. A knife that pierced deep in my heart. For many nights I cried behind that because I did whatever possible to make sure my daughter was not without a father, but this was how he treated me.

I could never really figure out why he hated me so much to the point I had to stop dealing with him, and only deal with the girlfriend. Funny right? I used to always blame myself for my relationships not working and I assumed that I did everything wrong and it was my fault that we didn't work. I became insecure and anger was my weapon of choice to defend myself. No one really understood me. Everyone assumed that it was because of my breakup the reason I acted the way I did, but nobody really knew me… the real me… the little hurt insecure girl that was trapped inside trying her best to get out so I could be free.

It took dating the wrong men, not loving myself, accepting anything from anybody to know I needed something different. I was invited to church only for the Pastor to preach about my life and the man didn't know a thing about me. I eventually ended up joining church and started to get my life back together. My faith in God had to increase in order for me to get to the point that I am at now.

I am nowhere near perfect and I still get tested daily, but now I know my worth and I don't depend on a man to tell me who I am because I know Whose I am. Giving my life back to God was challenging. Everything that could possibly go wrong did, but the only thing I had to hold on to was my faith; and because of my faith I am covered by God's grace and mercy. The only thing that I wish I would have done when I was younger was told my mother what my friends' uncle did to me that day. I'm a firm believer if I would have spoken up then my life probably would've been totally different now. A tough lesson learned.

Don't make the same mistake I did by keeping quiet. Years of bad decisions, unhealthy relationships, and wishing somebody would <u>see</u> the <u>real</u> me were all a result of that day in my friend's bedroom in the back of that apartment. Today, I take my life back. And now you see me. The real me.

Shon

The Frazier Chronicles

THE *Frazier* CHRONICLES

Section 2: Finding True Love

"To those who have given up on love, I say, trust life a little bit."
Maya Angelou

Chapter Eight

Angela R. Frazier

#theNewbie
Knight in Shining Armor

The Beginning. "I'm done with dating," I told my best friend over the phone as I sat on my couch and looked at my young son playing on the floor with his toys. "I'm done and over it...I just can't find a good, honest man. Why can't I find one that cares like me?" I cried into the phone softly, broken-hearted for the umpteenth time in my lifetime. I had no luck in finding a good partner.

It started in high school… the curse. Three years wasted on a high school crush only to break up with me the day before my birthday. My first break up. Then college, another long-term relationship full of verbal and physical abuse that almost cost me my life. I healed once again and moved on. Then, I thought I found love for real this time in an old acquaintance. Once again, another dud. To add insult to injury, he left me with a broken heart and a baby boy to raise on my own. This last and final straw that broke the camel's back was my last relationship. This guy pursued me relentlessly until I gave in. He really wasn't my type but I thought I could learn to love him, and I did. Then, I found out he was cheating on me.

I sat in my tiny apartment on the phone sobbing softly to my best friend of well over 10 years. "I just can't keep being a fool," I told her in a voice damp with tears and hurt. "I can't keep going on like this! I just…give up! I'm done dating, trying to find someone!" I'm angry now. I'm angry at myself for being so dumb and blind.

My friend responds, "Don't give up. There's someone out there for you. Watch, he will fall right into your lap." With a Kleenex tissue in hand, I wiped away my tears, cleared my throat, then asked, "Where is he then? I haven't met him yet." "Don't rush it," she says, "Listen, why don't we have a girl's night out?" I reluctantly agreed.

It's Saturday night and my best friend and I are on our way to the local "hole in the wall" club. I'm dressed in a satin purple thigh length dress with matching peep toed heels, hair cut in a bob, nails slayed to the gods, and makeup to match. We enter the club and I walk through the crowd of men as if I have the Midas touch. They swoon around me like I'm fresh meat and I decline each and every one of them nicely.

 Finally we make it to the bar, order our drinks and wait. I turn to scan the dance floor. Everyone seemed to be having a great time besides me. As I'm scanning, I met eyes with a stranger I've never seen before. He smiles a sweet smile at me to reveal a set of beautiful teeth. He had a smile that was full of boyish charm and it made me want to know him. My best friend tapped me on the shoulder breaking the trance I was in and hands me the drink. I smiled back at him shyly and walked away drink in hand.

 The night went on and, when it was time to leave at close time, we headed for the door. As the lights turned on, I'm walking and I get the feeling I'm being watched. Once again, I locked eyes with the stranger with the beautiful smile from across the room. We exchanged sweet smiles again and I exited through the door.

 My best friend ditches me so I ended up with a guy friend who spent the whole night with us talking about much of nothing. We decided to hit up the local wing spot, a common place the clubbers frequent during after party hours. We pull up to the wing spot and it's already packed…as usual. With my guy friend in tow, I push the door open and to my amazement, the stranger with the boyish smile and beautiful teeth is sitting at the bar. He's sitting there with a nice plaid button down shirt, a fitted hat, and nice Nike high tops to match. He smiles that boyish smile at me and asks me, "Are you following me?" I respond, "Nope, but you must be spying on me."

"My name is Terrence," he says. "I'm Angela," I respond. We carry on a conversation that includes light laughter and I completely forgot about my guy friend I came in with. A couple of minutes pass, we exchange numbers, say our goodbyes and I leave out the wing spot.

After a long night, I finally arrived home, took off my heels, checked in on my mom and son, then settled in on the couch to watch a little television. An hour later, I get a text from Terrence. He asked me if he could take me out to an early morning breakfast and, of course, I said 'yes'.

We ended up at IHOP. Took our seats, ordered our food, then began to talk about our lives. Terrence told me that he's never known his mother because she passed away shortly after giving birth to him due to labor complications. He told me the only mother he has ever known was his grandmother who raised him from birth. Although he was born in Louisiana, he was primarily raised in Mississippi, which makes him a good ole country boy. He was just so upfront and open about his life and this I liked.

I'm intrigued. Single, no kids, serving in the U.S. Air Force, and fine. My mind was screaming *something's wrong with this brutha*. I asked, "Why are you single?" His response captivated me even more, "I hadn't found the right one."

Next, it was my turn to share my life's events and many failed relationships, and so on. I'm usually not the type to open up about things but Terrence made me feel so comfortable. I said to him before taking a sip of my sweet tea, "I feel like I've known you forever." He smiled and we carried on our conversation until we noticed the sun started to shine through the restaurant window. I was in shock that so many hours had passed while we talked in IHOP. I was in awe.

We went back to my place to continue our conversation. Then Terrence dropped the question, "Do you have any kids?" I was reluctant to answer but I answered with a questionable "Yes?" He then said, "Oh, so is it a boy or a girl?" I told him I had a little boy. As soon as those words rolled off my lips I heard a "bump, bump, bump" sound. I think to myself, *Why are you up right now little boy?!*

Here comes Jordan, my one-year-old at the time wearing footie pajamas sliding down the steps backwards on his belly. He ran over to me and then noticed someone else was in the house. He looked at Terrence, walked over to him and started playing with him. I'm shocked. My son had never taken to any male like that. We all spent the rest of the day playing with each other and watching movies.

The First Few Years. "I don't know what I'm going to do without you here with me," I said choking back tears, not wanting to cry in front of Terrence. "You'll be fine without me," he said.

I asked him, "Are you breaking up with me because you're deploying?" He didn't answer. It was a hot day in May as we sat in the laundry room folding clothes. I sat on top of the dryer while Terrence stood in between my legs as we talked on this sensitive subject of deployment.

"I love you," I said…it just came out of nowhere. My true feelings had spilled out and overflowed everywhere. That was it, I was an emotional wreck.

"I love you, too," Terrence replied, "we will work through this while I'm gone, we can do it." I was on cloud nine. We hugged and I cried some more. He told me he didn't want to be like those other guys, deploy and then come home to nothing, woman gone with all of their stuff and another man, left heartbroken. I told him, "I ain't going nowhere; I'll be here when you get back." We hugged and kissed and I felt safe and at ease.

The weeks to come we spent as much time together. We went out to dinner, took long walks together, and took Jordan to the park to play. Terrence was my dream guy. I had never felt love for anyone else in the past the way I felt it for him. Just to hear his voice on the phone just made me giddy like a little school girl. I would get chills when he touched my skin. Everything about him was just magical. I loved him, I needed him, and I breathed him. He was all I ever could want in my life. He was my King.

Six months later and the end of the deployment had come. Terrence was coming home! I've waited for this moment to see his face again. Of course, I couldn't sleep the night before, anticipating all kinds of things… how he would look, did he still love me, has deployment changed the man I loved. I was just so excited and nervous at the same time. The drive to the airport to pick up Terrence was the longest ever!

I couldn't get there fast enough. I'm at the gate, waiting impatiently to see that face. Then I saw those distinct ears and that special walk coming through the crowd. I made my way through the crowd to greet him before he cleared the aisle of people. I jumped into his arms nearly taking him down and we kissed for what seemed like eternity. It was just magical. I cried and people were applauding because the sentiment was just mutual—a man that served his country had made it home!

As our relationship blossomed, the years count away. We'd gone through a deployment and several TDY's (temporary duty). One day out of the blue we started talking about marriage. We just randomly talked about how it would be if we were married and the life changes to expect. He asked if I thought marriage was something I thought I could do. My response was YES!

As a little girl, I'd always dreamed about how it would be to be married to that dream guy with 2.5 kids, a dog, and a beautiful home with a well-manicured lawn with a white picket fence. Of course, once getting into my adult years I knew that marriage was nothing of the sort, but still I was willing and wanting to dedicate my life and love to one person only for the rest of my natural life.

The Wedding Day. November 30, 2012 was an absolute horrible day at work and I swear that I wanted to quit right there on the spot! My feet were aching from walking from building to building, hall to hall running STAT bloodwork back and forth. My back was aching from all the hard sticks on patients. I could not believe the number of patients I had seen on that day that veins were a challenge (I was a phlebotomist). By the time 5:30 p.m. came around, I was worn out and ready to go home and chill out!

Terrence was home waiting on me and he told me that his co-workers were having a get together at the Bleu Café' (my favorite restaurant) and invited us. I said, "I'm too tired to get dressed up, I've had a horrible day. You can go without me." That was a "no go" for Terrence and he then pleads with me to go so, again, reluctantly I give in. I showered and put on a little black and grey dress with black strappy heels to match. My feet were really killing me now. I put on my makeup, popped in my contacts, and we were out the door. My mom was watching Jordan for me and said that they were going out to grab a bite to eat with my sister later.

Terrence and I pulled up at the restaurant. I told him that I'd rather not be out too long because I was just exhausted from work. We walked hand in hand up the sidewalk into the restaurant. Everyone warmly greeted us with hugs and smiles. Terrence walked me to the head of the table and pulled out my chair. Feeling uneasy about having the spotlight seat, I take a seat. Everyone was mingling, drinking, listening to the live band, and enjoying the ambience throughout the whole restaurant. I was in a full conversation with one of his co-workers when my mother, son, and sister walked in. I began to sweat. Shocked and surprised, I asked, "What are y'all doing here?" "We were invited," they responded. Okay, now something is fishy here.

Everyone was seated and Terrence stood up, tapped a wine glass to get everyone's attention, then looked at me. The doorman brought out a bouquet of red roses and handed them to me. I smiled. Terrence continued to talk, repeating himself twice thus making my mom snap out of her daze to bring him a suede black box. He kneeled down on one knee, opened the ring box and asked me to marry him. Of course, I was floored as I was standing there and everyone was chanting and I screamed out, "YES! A million times YES!" He placed a beautiful princess cut vintage style ring onto my left ring finger. He stood, we kissed, and everyone in the restaurant stood up applauding. I swore in that moment I forgot my feet were hurting because I was on cloud one million.

In the weeks to come we were into wedding planning. We chose to be married on May 25, 2013 so that left us with six months to get the ball rolling. We hired a wedding planner immediately. We talked venues and finally settled on an old plantation mansion in town called The Crescent Garden Center.

The evening before was wedding rehearsals at the venue. Our out-of-town family were now there with us. Terrence' older brother was a groomsmen in the wedding. Unbeknownst to Terrence we were expecting an extra guest, Terrence's oldest brother whom he hadn't seen since he was about eight years old. Terrence was shocked. It was an emotional moment. They embraced for what seemed like a lifetime. My heart felt warm. We casually talked after rehearsal and then parted ways until the next day…our wedding day.

Long time coming and I couldn't believe it was my wedding day!! On edge, I hopped out of the bed in the hotel room. My best friend and my cousin were all giddy. I screamed, "I'm getting married today!" We each took turns to shower then headed over to check on the reception hall and the wedding venue. Everything looked perfect. My wedding planner was running the show and not playing any games. By 1:30 p.m., it was full on chaos! I was hyperventilating and in a panic. Nothing was going right and my damn hostess was MISSING!!!! Everyone was in my suite trying to calm me down but it wasn't working.

After my mini meltdown, I was scuffled over by my matron of honor, my bestie, to get my hair and makeup done. I started to feel a little better. Back to the suite so I could get dressed with my mother and photographer in the room. As my wedding planner was lacing up the back of my dress it hit me, *This is really happening. I'm really about to get married.*

I was finally dressed. My mother gave me something borrowed, she hugged me so tight and said she loved me then kissed me on the cheek. I was teary eyed at that moment but I fought back tears. I told her that I loved her too then returned the hug and kiss.

I was not allowed to sit down once I had my dress on so I had to rely on two of my bridesmaids to hold me up while my wedding planner placed on my feet Ivory Christian Louboutins that I received as a pre-wedding gift from my fiancé'. My matron of honor then put on my cathedral length veil and I felt like a princess. I looked at myself in a body length mirror while the photographer captured that moment. I felt blessed, loved, just every happy emotion was running through my veins and through my soul. I was ready!

I was escorted down the staircase and out the backdoor. The horse drawn carriage was waiting for me. The driver took my hand and helped me into the carriage while my matron of honor guided my train into the carriage behind me. My veil was drawn as I sat holding my live bouquet of flowers nervously. The carriage driver steered the carriage to a neighborhood street away from the guests to wait for the phone call from the wedding coordinator. I sat in the beautiful sunshine awaiting the moment. People came out of their homes to look and to congratulate me on my upcoming nuptials.

Finally, the carriage driver phone rang. It's time! He yanked the reins and the horses went into a polite trot. The people standing on their porches started to clap and wave as we rode off. I waved in return and took in a deep breath. We finally made it onto the main road. Cars were honking and people were pulling over and shouting "congratulations!" I felt like I was in a fairy tale. We were approaching the venue; I could hear the violinist playing faintly. "Click, clack" the sound of the horses hooves on the street. We had finally arrived at the walkway. Everyone in attendance was standing and I could hear the "oooo's" and the "ahhhh's".

My uncle was at the walkway to help me down and to escort me down the aisle. I saw Terrence standing at the altar with the biggest smile on his face and I began to cry out of joy. My uncle patted my hand and whispered to me that it was okay and to focus on us walking. We walked to the rhythm of the violinist tune until we reached the altar. My uncle hugged me and gave me over to my soon-to-be husband. I took Terrence's hand and he guided me up the stairs to the altar. We exchanged vows and rings as we both smiled uncontrollably. We then each sealed our bond as a family of three by me, Terrence, and Jordan pouring unity sand into one single jar.

Right there we stood, in the warm May sun in front of family, friends, and God, and gave our souls to each other forever and ever more. Terrence removed my veil from my face and placed a kiss on my lips that took my breath away. It was official. We were presented to the crowd as Mr. & Mrs. Terrence D. Frazier!

So much love and joy swam through my soul that I was elated. I screamed out comically "I's married now!" and the crowd laughed. We stepped down from the altar and walked hand in hand down the aisle as the crowd blew bubbles onto us. Our horse and carriage awaited us at the end of the aisle. I stepped up into the carriage with the help of the carriage driver and my husband in tow. We waved to the crowd one last time before we headed off to the reception venue.

My husband and I have grown together over the years. We now have a second son together and we are still enjoying each other through the good and bad. Here's my message: Never give up on love… God may let you test the waters and experience heartache and pain, but that fish is still out there waiting on you, so stop trying to catch it. Let that fish naturally come to you.

Angie

Special Note from Terrence

Son of Yolanda, Raised by Minnie Lee O'Neal (Frazier) after Yolanda's demise

Hi everybody! My name is Terrence D. Frazier, and I'm stopping by to share how I became appreciative to what I've come to recognize as *true love*.

You see… I am a member of the United States Air Force and, for most of us, when we reach our first duty station, we are usually miles and miles away from our immediate family. So we all know how this starts off for some of us: when we get to the first duty station, someone takes you out, introduces you to a few people, and before you know it, you've established connections and now you're wilding out every weekend (that means partying hard).

Well, a few years and relationships go by, and I'm starting to mature. I'm getting to the point where I occasionally go out, and when I do, I'm not indulging in conversation just based off of outward looks, but I'm checking her third eye—in other words I'm checking her intellect. I'm checking to see if we are on the same wavelength… is she someone that I need to catch up to or are we that perfect match to where we balance each other out— where we can teach each other and grow together equally.

Fast forward, on one of the light occasions where I'm stepping out with the crew, I spot this beautiful brown-skinned woman. If my memory serves me right, she was wearing this dark olive green dress. I think I must've eyed her the whole night, but I didn't talk to her then. She was baaaad though! Fine as hell!

But, the weird thing was that me and the crew decided to hit up this food joint after the club, called Andy's, and no one went in except for me. So I'm in line to order my food and in comes the baddest chick I had seen earlier that night in the club… with another guy. I waited until he walked off and that's when I talked to her. Come to find out they weren't together, and from then on we were inseparable!

Fast forward again about two years or so, and we're still dating. Now I'm thinking ring. Not just any ring, I'm talking THE RING, but still not 100% yet. Then my duty station get hit with a 6-month deployment to the sand box. To myself I'm thinking, *This will be my test. If we can withstand distance and make it, then surely she can withstand being a military spouse.*

Six months passed and I proposed. The very next work day, I get orders to Kunsan AB, Republic of Korea for 12 months! WOW!!! Another test had gone by and we survived, but this time we were married. So now it's 2016 and I recently received orders to go to Osan AB, Republic of Korea. I've come to realize that this is not a test anymore. This is the life that God has given us as Mr. and Mrs. Frazier.

Angie, you are the best mother, homie, lover, friend, supporter and military spouse that any military husband could ever want and need! There is no one else that I would rather spend it with than Mrs. Angela R. Frazier. And for that, I thank you!

For everyone else, here's my take on it: to have a successful relationship, or just be successful in general, you have to have a successful support system — in hopes that you choose your other half <u>as</u> your support system.

If your support system is not healthy you need to rethink what you're doing. On the other hand, if you're supporting someone and not receiving healthy support in return, then you need to rethink what you're doing. And that's coming from a man's point of view.

Section 3: When Life Unexpectedly Throws You a Curve Ball

"Nobody's perfect I may not be the most beautiful, the sexiest, or the girl with the perfect body, but I don't pretend to be someone I'm not. I am good at being me." Unknown

Chapter Nine

Sharalene D. Frazier

#LovingMe
In My Skin

Growing up for me was fun. I can't really remember anything that was bad about it. I had four older brothers and four older sisters, making me the ninth child; yet, when I was 21-years-old, my father died and my whole life changed.

My relationship with my mother went down hill and I turned to men as a means of comfort. However, I had somewhat of a desire to be with women also. I lived a secret life for years and it was after I had three children that I decided to come out to my family about my sexuality.

When my children were very young, I began to openly date women. All of those relationships were target. I found myself in the same situations like I was when I was with men. Some were emotionally draining and others were violent. During my whirlwind of bad relationships, being a single parent and being a member of a very dysfunctional family, I began to get very depressed.

I lived with my mother and every day, all day, she would put me down and talk badly about me, constantly beating down my self-esteem and tearing my life apart with all of her negative words. I was very angry and broken and had a really hard time trying to function in life. On the bright side, though, I always had really great jobs; and in the mist of all my mess, I completed Licensed Practical Nurse (LPN) school.

With my new career it seemed as if I would start to look at things differently, but for a while things got worse. After finishing school, I still chose to hang out with all the wrong people. One relationship after the other, not ever finding any peace. I felt like life wasn't worth living. Then one day after the most unforgettable fights ever, I had some really bad thoughts and considered doing some really bad things to myself. I was at my wits end. I had had enough.

I got a phone call from a friend and I told her my plans, she told me to stay still and soon after her mother came over and took me and my children to her house where I was offered salvation. Soon after, I joined church and became a devout

Christian, very seldom missing a Sunday, and living my life the way the world thought I should live it. But secretly and unknowingly, I was still unfulfilled. I guess you can say I was just existing. Still trying to find my way, even in this newfound Christian living thing.

For nine long years, I was single and waiting on God, so I thought. I spent many lonely nights when finally my hormones kicked in and I fell from grace, as the church folks would say. While at work, I met a young lady and soon after we became friends. We began to hang out together and spent a lot of time together, but it wasn't very long before things got out of hand. She and I became intimate.

She would spend most days at my house with me and my children. My children were very young so I didn't feel the need to try to explain our relationship to them, however she was a stud and wore men clothing… it wasn't hard for them to figure it out. My two boys had nothing bad to say about it, but my daughter, on the other hand, was ashamed of me. She told me that she didn't like my friend and that she didn't want her around any more. I honestly struggled with that but I thought that I should be happy for once so I continued to allow my friend to come around.

My relationship with my daughter went to hell, she didn't ever want to be home nor did she want to be around me. I struggled with that every day. My daughter hated my friend and turned to my God-sister for support. For a while I allowed her to be disrespectful by talking back to me and go over to my God-sister's house whenever she wanted. But it wasn't long before I found out that this new friend of mine wasn't right for me and that she wasn't worth me losing my family for... but by then it was too late. My daughter hated me and I allowed this woman to tear up my whole family.

My relationship with my daughter was never the same after that failed relationship with my friend, even though I told her that she was important to me and how much I loved her. She constantly reminded me of choosing somebody over her... my life has never been the same even though I tried to rid this ex-lover out of my life, she would constantly come around. During our relationship, she formed a relationship with my boys and they continued communication after the break-up. It wasn't long after that my daughter decided she wanted to stay with her father.

I tried all I could to keep my daughter with me but our fights were getting worse. She talked to her dad and he decided that it was best for her to stay with him. When my daughter left to go stay with her dad, I felt that I had lost her forever. I was so heart broken and destroyed. I felt like my life was over.

Today, two years later, I'm in a new relationship and my relationship with my daughter is better. We text and sometimes she calls, but it's not where a mother and daughter relationship should be. I'm most grateful that she even talks to me.

What I learned from all that I've been through is never let your children date who you date. There should be limitations on what you allow them to see you go through. Never let your children feel like they are not important to you and always keep them close. I lost my daughter because I chose what I thought would make me happy. I spent nine whole years dedicated to pleasing them and when I decided to do something for me, it was the wrong decision. I lost my relationship with my daughter because I was so desperate to find myself. Honestly, I really believe I went through all of that because of my damaged relationship with my own mother. All of her negativity affected my self-esteem and self-worth, forcing me on this long journey to find myself. I've made some mistakes along the way. As I look back, I wonder was it truly worth it?

I'm still struggling with who I am. Every so often I feel I've let my daughter down. I have a wonderful relationship with my boys and I'm still praying that one day my daughter would see that I love her too. She is the most beautiful part of me. I know that now.

Sharalene

"Our greatest glory is not in never falling, but in getting up every time we do." Unknown

Chapter Ten

Shanelle D. Frazier

#SmilingonPurpose
Two's a Crowd

W ho knew that a misdiagnosis of muscle spasms would turn a girl's world upside down? Hi, I'm Shanelle. My entire life has revolved around being known as the girl who always smiles. Everybody knows my personality, always happy and joyous, and such a people person. I hail from a small town in the Mississippi Delta, where everybody knows everybody. What is something else that we all know about small towns…there is not much to do? And so the story begins.

THE *Frazier* CHRONICLES

Growing up in the 90s, I kept myself busy by staying active, you know, doing what it is that kids do: playing outside, riding my bicycle and just running around being a kid. In school, I was a cheerleader and track runner too. I was a very petite child and would always get teased for being skinny. But I used it to my advantage at times. My favorite pastime was cheerleading.

Cheerleading was my life! From being at cheerleading practice, to cheering at the football and basketball games and doing stunts. For those that may be unfamiliar with cheerleading lingo, I was a fly girl, meaning I was the girl that was held up and thrown in the air during stunts. Some critics do not look at cheerleading as a sport, but it is an intense sport and people can get hurt just like they would on a court or field. It was through cheerleading, my passion, that I discovered a problem.

I would sometimes experience random and unusual pains on my left side. They would come all of a sudden. This started to happen at about the age of 13 or 14. The pain would be very intense and only last minutes, then just stop. It was weird to me, because it would only happen a few times a year. I used to just shrug it off. By the middle of year two is when I decided that I should probably tell my mother about it. My mother then started asking all of these questions. I'm pretty sure that we all know how mothers are. Anyway, the next stop was the doctor visit.

I went to the same local medical clinic that I had been going pretty much my entire life. I remember the visit just like it was yesterday. We enter the clinic, sign in, my mom takes care of the paperwork and then we wait. After a while, we are finally called to the back to wait in a room for the doctor.

After a few moments, Dr. White walked in. We explained the purpose for the visit. Dr. White did his normal checks of the ear, nose and throat and then used his stethoscope to listen to my breathing. He pressed on my left side where I said that I had been experiencing the pain. He pressed and felt around and then proceeded to ask me to move around and do certain exercises to make a determination as to what was going on. I jumped up and down and just constantly moved around for a few moments, but I was not experiencing any pain while being in the office with my mother and the doctor. He asked if I did a lot of physical activity, and we gave as much specifics as we could. After the examination, Dr. White diagnosed me with muscle spasms and ordered a prescription for muscle relaxers. With cheerleading and track and just being a kid, my mother and I thought it sounded right and were looking to just put this ailment behind us.

Life went on for me. I continued to cheer and do all of the things that I used to do before the doctor visit. Over the years, the "muscle spasms" would come and go, and I would take the muscle relaxers when I could remember. It got to a point though where I stopped taking them altogether because the spasms did not occur frequent enough to somewhat matter to me. Yes, they were painful, but the pain didn't last long enough to deal with the hassle of it all. I guess you can say that I just got used to the pain. It was something that happened, and I was just dealing with it.

In my going to the doctor for other ailments such as a cold or some sort of injury, I would mention to Dr. White that I was still having those pains in my side, and even when I would take the muscle relaxers, I could not tell a big difference. My question was, would this pain ever go away? But, at that point, no one had a definite answer. His diagnosis remained the same.

Little did I know that February 2007, news from my doctor would change my outlook on some things. I had a scheduled appointment with my gynecologist, Dr. Taylor, for my annual check-up. In my mind, it would be just a normal day with normal results. I'm sitting in the waiting room and I'm finally called to the back for the standard tests prior to going to see my doctor, after which I'm sent to yet another waiting room. Finally, I heard my name and it was time to go in to the room to wait for my doctor to come in and perform the examination.

Dr. Taylor came in with her warm and welcoming smile as usual. She asked if there was anything wrong or if I had any questions about anything and I answered, "No Ma'am." She then proceeded with the examination. During the examination, she looked at my stomach and said, "Shanelle, your tummy looks rather bloated, is this normal?"

To me, it looked normal. At that point, I was 20-years-old and not as small as I used to be, but I was not very big either. I always had what some called a little "pooch" for a stomach, but it wasn't noticeable. I told her that my stomach always looked that way, and I didn't think anything of it. She then pressed down on my stomach and abdominal area. While examining that area, Dr. Taylor had a peculiar look on her face which immediately made me scared. She then said, "I don't remember your abdominal area feeling like this before, it feels very hard. I want to do some further testing."

My mouth dropped! My emotions immediately went to fear, doubt and worry. In that second, I wanted my mother by my side, but I was old enough to visit the doctor alone. When I came back to reality, I asked her what she thought it could be and what was going to happen to me? I just asked any and everything that I could because I could not believe that something could be wrong with me. Dr. Taylor said, "I will not know for sure until we do more testing, but you may have fibroids." "Fibroids!" I yelled out. I had maybe heard that term before but did not know what it meant or what it would do to me. Dr. Taylor scheduled me for further testing two weeks later. At that point, I had heard enough, I just wanted to get out of there and get to my mom and loved ones for some support.

Those next two weeks of waiting were tough. Crying and worrying had overtaken the girl who was known for always smiling. We did not know what was wrong and the waiting and guessing just added stress to me. I found out that a family member had to have surgery to get her fibroids removed, so I started to think that could also be me. What really kept me going was the strength and prayers from my mother and my darling grandmother. You see, I was young, but I did know God. Sudden news that I had just received had caused my faith to be shaken, but it never left. I had to remember that God said that He would never put more on us than we could bear, and I was doing all of this worrying, not even knowing my fate. I had to get it together.

Two weeks later, I returned for my appointment. I found out that I had to have a hysteroscopy—a procedure that allows doctors to look through the vagina and inspect. After the procedure, I was told that I would have to wait on the results. Sometime later, I was called in to receive my results. I made sure to take my mother with me for the news. Dr. Taylor came in with her usual smile. She told me that what she saw from the exam and testing was a pelvic mass. She said it appeared to be about the size of a grapefruit. The next thing that I heard from her was SURGERY. Again, my mind wandered off and I began to think about being cut open, risks, what if something goes wrong, and then I thought about the scar that it would leave. Sadness came upon me.

My mind was all over the place, when I snapped out of it, I realized that my mom was doing all of the talking for me and just asking all of the important questions that I could not think of, and asking about options. Dr. Taylor actually suggested a second opinion from another gynecologist that worked at the facility who was known as an excellent surgeon. I was still a bit shocked from the news and now I was hearing that I might have to change doctors, and my new doctor was a "he". At that moment, I could not allow that to bother me, we needed to take care of me and figure out the next steps, so we agreed to meet with the other gynecologist.

The next appointment came about a week later. As my mother and I—yes, I brought my mother back to the doctor with me—were waiting in the room, Dr. Patel, the new doctor walked in. Dr. Patel is well known for not only being an amazing doctor and surgeon, but also for being very personable and caring. Of course you know that I did my research!

After the meet and greet, Dr. Patel got right down to business. He examined me, looked over my charts, and agreed with Dr. Taylor. He also wanted to schedule the surgery as soon as possible, May 2007 to be exact. And thus we began pre-operation procedures—from getting my first IV (intravenous fluid drip), a CAT scan, blood work, more doctor visits, completed paper work and, yes, more tests. I was a junior in college so scheduling the surgery in May worked out perfectly because I would be on summer break. Not to mention it was also scheduled after my twenty-first birthday! As you can see, I had my priorities in order!

The night before the surgery, I had to do a little preparation which consisted of drinking a solution to clean out my system. Let's just say I hope to never experience that again! I also had to refrain from consuming liquids or foods after midnight. I talked with family and friends to help ease my mind. I prayed and hoped for a successful surgery. I did not sleep much, but I didn't think it mattered since I would be given anesthesia before Dr. Patel performed the laparotomy procedure.

I arrived on time, 6:00 a.m., and was escorted back to a room for Pre-Op. My mom was right there by my side while the nurses prepared me for surgery. I was in better spirits due to the phone calls, texts and prayers from family and friends just that same morning. I knew that no matter what happened, my people loved me, and God had His hands on me.

It was now surgery time! Dr. Patel came in with a smile and was very encouraging. He reassured me that everything would be okay and that I was in good hands. I remember lying on the gurney and being rolled towards the operating room when Dr. Patel asked me to start counting backwards from one hundred.

Okay, let's pause for a moment. I was determined to prove that the medicine to put me to sleep was not that strong. I saw in movies and heard from other people that you would be "knocked out" quickly, and you wouldn't even know it. So, I started counting... 100, 99, 98... and the next memory that I had was waking up in a room surrounded by family and friends.

When I woke up from the surgery, I immediately smiled because I survived it, and to see family and friends there for me made my heart smile. Nurses were in and out that day checking vitals and making sure that I was comfortable. My family and myself included were waiting on Dr. Patel to come in to give us prayerfully some good news. Finally, Dr. Patel arrived, again with a smile on his face, and stated that the surgery went well, but there were details that we needed to know.

The pelvic mass was successfully removed, but it was not the size of a grapefruit in which they had initially suggested. It was much larger. The mass weighed about ten pounds and was huge. It was so huge, that the median incision that Dr. Patel made had to be longer to remove the mass. Not only that, but the mass was located on my left side, where I was experiencing the pain all of those years, and it encompassed my left ovary, which in turn had to be removed as well.

Once again, this was a lot to take in and process, and I was in a state of shock. I was very grateful to be alive and to have had a successful surgery, but when I heard that I lost an ovary, my mind immediately went to my ability to conceive. Here I was a 21-year-old woman with no children and now I had to think about the possibility of maybe never having children. I was sad, I was mad, I was hurt. Even though I had not expressed it, I had always wanted to have children. Being a mother was my dream and now it was threatened by this mass thing!

After that meltdown, I had to come back to reality and stop jumping the gun. I asked Dr. Patel about my chances of having children. He stated that my right ovary was healthy, and as long as it was good, I would be fine. I had not imagined ever that I would be sitting in a hospital and having to ask the burning question, "Will I be able to have children?"

Even through all of that, Dr. Patel was not done. The pelvic mass that was removed was called a dermoid cyst (teratoma) which had apparently been with me since birth. After removing the mass, they examined it and found hair, teeth, skin and other particles on the inside of it. Dr. Patel said to me that for 21 years, I had been carrying my twin on the inside of me. All I could think was, "WOW!!"

Other doctors and researchers have determined that the dermoid cyst, being considered the twin, is an old wives' tale, but I do believe that it definitely could have been mine. My mom's dad was a twin and no one else in the family conceived twins, so they believed that it was my mother who was supposed to have them. The results from the surgery confirm that she was supposed to as well.

Also while examining the mass, tissues were sent to a lab to make sure that it was benign or considered non-cancerous. The little energy that I had left after all of that news was used to just wait and pray. After a three-day, two-night stay in the hospital, I left with a flatter and scarred tummy, one ovary, results that the pelvic mass was benign, and a healthy report that, God willing, I would be able to conceive.

The healing process was a six weeks process. My mother took care of me and would not allow me to even wash my hair, or pick up anything, or leave the house for the entire six weeks. Old school mothers…got to love them! I spent my days taking my post surgery antibiotics, keeping my incision clean, coping with all of the news from the surgery and preparing to go to summer school. After my six weeks recovery period, I attended summer school and got back to life. I was ready to begin August 2007 as a senior in college.

Since the surgery, I have not had any post-surgery complications. Over the years though, I have suffered with issues relating to abnormal test results after visiting my gynecologist, but after further testing and treatment, I am still in the clear of being healthy and able to conceive. By the way, Dr. Patel is still my gynecologist. We have a great doctor/patient relationship. He often jokes and asks me when I am going to give him a baby (to deliver of course), and I do recognize the seriousness of the situation due to my medical history and my age.

I am now 30 years old, and I still do not have children. Let me also say that I have not been trying to have children either. Currently, I am a single female with a desire to be married and to be a mother. *I may have lost an ovary, but I will not lose my faith.*

Do I wonder 'what if'? Do I get scared? Do I worry? Do I pray? The answer to all of these questions is YES! I am human.

With my heart, I believe that no matter what, God's Will will be done for my life, and I have to accept it. I am going to accept it. Through all I have gone through, it only made me stronger. I could not see that then because I was too young and my walk with Christ was not where it is today. I now know that God used me, because He knew that I could handle it, and that I would be able to help someone in a similar situation to get through it.

What really keeps me smiling through the doubt and pain is that God has still given me a chance. I still have a chance to receive a desire of my heart and that is to have children. He could have easily taken that option away from me, but He didn't. A chance is good enough for me, and I am very grateful. Doctors say that the older you wait to conceive, the higher the risk, and I do follow doctor's orders, but God's Word will always trump what man says. Keep the faith and never give up.

Social norms say that a person who is not married or does not have children by a certain age is an outcast. For those in my category—30+, single, no children, whether it be by choice or by force—we don't follow social norm, we follow God's Word. His Word says that He will give us the desires of our heart, and that He will never leave us nor forsake us. If you believe that, there is nothing that you cannot do or overcome. We are going to make it!! Keep the faith, and keep smiling!!

Shanelle

THE *Frazier* CHRONICLES

Final Note from the Authors

 Thank you for reading our story in our OWN words, in our OWN voice! But, here is the REAL takeaway: You are NOT alone!!! The women in our family SUFFERED great and long. We kept many SECRETS. We kept much pain INSIDE. We lived most of our lives in an indescribable pain that you may never be able to imagine. But, all of that was for this very moment: To SURVIVE in order to EXPOSE the TRUTH of what happens in the DARK, and to FREE others so they will NOT have to suffer the way we did.

 There is one thing that got us all through: **FAITH**. And there is one thing that keeps us moving forward: **FORGIVENESS**.

 Once you learn the key and secret to faith and forgiveness, your life will never be the same.

Love you to life,

The Frazier Women

Afterword

To sum it all up, this journey of telling our story to be emotionally healed has been a challenging process. Looking back at the women in our family, even those who opted <u>out</u> of joining this anthology project, the great Maya Angelou's poem, *Still I Rise*, comes to mind.

We hope something we have shared has inspired you to choose life, you are NOT alone, you are worth saving, and you are worth loving. Join us on our healing journey, and let's be healed together. Together, we rise.

The Frazier Chronicles

About the Publisher

Jamie Y. Hopkins (formerly Timmons), also known as Jai, is the Founder of Jai the Author Publishing, and is a best-selling author, blogger, radio show host and visionary. In 2014, she released her first memoir, It Is Forbidden: The Untold Story of Child Rape Survival, and has spent a good amount of time and resources empowering others to tell their story and be free from the pain of it.

She founded the parent company, Matters of My Heart, LLC, of which Jai the Author Publishing is a subsidiary. Matters of My Heart, LLC houses an emotional support program for adult survivors of child domestic and sexual abuse, and aides in the transition from a place of hurt to emotional healing. Jai's message is, "**My past does not define me, it refines me.**"

Holding a dual graduate degree in International Management and Masters of Business Administration (MBA), Jai has travelled to Kenya, Tanzania, Uganda, Indonesia and Cambodia to conduct research with government officials and children affected by the worst forms of child labor, including child trafficking. This travel has broadened her senses to different cultures and lifestyles; and has created a deep respect to all mankind, with all ethnicity and backgrounds.

The pain of Jai's past has developed into a passion to help others like her, realizing there are people hurting all over the world. Her purpose in life is to be the voice of the child (boy or girl) who is being abused by someone they know, yet they do not have the wherewithal to verbalize the abuse. Jai declares, "I will continue the fight to bring awareness to what is done in the dark, expose the ugly truths, and create an environment of healing for the hurt."

Her focus now is to partner with organizations with the same mission. Jai strongly believes in partnership. "Together, we can eliminate domestic violence and sexual assault in this world!" As such, Jai is a member of the Speaker Bureau for the Rape, Abuse & Incest National Network (RAINN), the nation's largest anti-sexual assault organization, where she also staffs the National Sexual Assault Hotline.

Learn more about Jai's emotional support program operated by Matters of My Heart, LLC at www.mattersofmyheart.com

Learn more about Jai's self-publishing company at http://jaitheauthor.com

Purchase other books by Jai at amazon.com/author/jai

If you, or someone you know, is being abused, please call the National Domestic Violence Hotline at 1-800-799-SAFE (7233), or visit http://www.thehotline.org to chat live with a victim advocate (available 24/7, confidential and anonymous).

If you, or someone you know, has been sexually assaulted, please call the National Sexual Assault Hotline at 1-800-656-HOPE (4673), or visit https://www.rainn.org to chat live with a victim advocate (available 24/7, confidential and anonymous).

www.ingramcontent.com/pod-product-compliance
Lightning Source LLC
Chambersburg PA
CBHW072056290426
44110CB00014B/1709